T0116281

ALSO BY MARTHA TOD DUDMAN

Augusta, Gone

EXPECTING TO FLY

A SIXTIES RECKONING

MARTHA TOD DUDMAN

SIMON & SCHUSTER

New York • London • Toronto • Sydney

SIMON & SCHUSTER
Rockefeller Center
1230 Avenue of the Americas
New York, NY 10020

Copyright © 2004 by Martha Tod Dudman
All rights reserved,
including the right of reproduction
in whole or in in part in any form.

SIMON & SCHUSTER AND COLOPHON ARE REGISTERED TRADEMARKS
OF SIMON & SCHUSTER, INC.

This is essentially a work of nonfiction. However, many names and details
of the characters have been changed, and some events and characters
have been conflated or fictionalized.

For information about special discounts for bulk purchases,
please contact Simon & Schuster Special Sales:
1-800-456-6798 or business@simonandschuster.com

Manufactured in the United States of America

10   8   6   4   2   1   3   5   7   9

Library of Congress Cataloging-in-Publication Data
Dudman, Martha Tod.
Expecting to fly : a sixties reckoning / Martha Tod Dudman.
    p.   cm.
1. Dudman, Martha Tod—Childhood and youth. 2. United States—History—1961–1969.
3. Washington Region—Biography. 4. Women—United States—Biography. I. Title.
CT275.D876626A3 2004
973.923'092—dc22   2003065665

ISBN-10: 1-4165-6811-5
ISBN-13: 978-1-4165-6811-7

My thanks to
SUSAN TAYLOR CHEHAK, CONSTANCE HUNTING,
BETSY LERNER, CANDICE STOVER,
and especially DENISE ROY
for their encouragement
and sound advice.

EXPECTING TO FLY

PROLOGUE

I WASN'T AT WOODSTOCK, but Danny was. I knew that the way you always knew key information about people. Where they were when Kennedy was shot. If they would have gone to Vietnam or Canada. If they'd taken acid. How many times—a lot or just the once. If they'd been to Woodstock.

I'd been at the Ann Arbor Blues Festival that hot summer weekend in 1969; hitched up with Mark from Yellow Springs and camped out in a field. We were pretty stoned all weekend. Windowpane.

🌀

Years later everything was different. I was married and had a couple of babies; reading *Redbook* magazine and baking bread. Every Sunday I visited my grandmother at the nursing home. My husband worked nights at the radio station. It snowed every day that winter.

One night it was quiet in the house and the snow was falling. I turned on the television and flipped through the three channels we could get in Northeast Harbor in 1984 and came across the movie *Woodstock* playing on public television.

I kept the sound down low so it wouldn't wake the children and I watched *Woodstock*. God. I'd forgotten how we looked back then. Our hair! Our torn jeans. Our velvet shirts. Our enormous earrings. Our floppy breasts. Our hair our hair our hair. I saw the young girls with their smooth full cheeks, their doughy innocence. I was like that too, then; innocent and young. They were throwing themselves around in wild dances. I used to do that too. I couldn't dance enough.

Oh I remembered that now, sitting in my own home in Maine with my flannel nightgown and my babies in their beds and my house around me and my husband up in Ellsworth playing Frank Sinatra on WDEA. Which part was the dream? Which part was real?

How had I become this—cutting out coupons for the Shop 'N Save. Going to lunches with other mothers who weren't anything at all like me. And what happened to all that?

All that time, all that excitement, all that feeling of being at the center of things, all that sense of justification and deliverance and magical power—all that reduced to muddy kids dancing in the cow pies and young musicians dead now with their beautiful, angelic faces and their frantic, lost guitars.

When I turned the television off I wasn't exactly crying, but I felt a dim and hollow feeling. How it was.

I wanted to talk to someone who had been there too.

I knew where Danny lived in California. Over the years, after we'd broken up and gone our different ways, we'd kept in touch, calling each other every couple of years, sending Christmas cards with pictures of our children. I still got his mother's annual holiday report with her familiar slanted handwriting. A photo of the Greene family on some trip; white-water rafting in Colorado, traveling through Nepal, atop the Alps.

❧

His voice is still familiar. I hope I don't sound like one of those drunk women calling years later lonely in their lonely houses. I'm not like that. I'm okay. I just want something.

"I was just watching *Woodstock,*" I tell him.

"Oh yeah?"

"I don't know. I just wanted to talk to you. I mean, do you ever think about all that? About how it was? I mean, wasn't there something sort of magical about that time? We were onto some kind of a religious experience or something? Like, weren't we part of something? I don't know. I mean I don't go around thinking about it. I just—I remember how it was then. That feeling we had."

I run out of steam. Beside me the cold window is black with the black night beyond. I can see my face reflected in the glass. I look the same, I think, but I look older.

"You know," he says finally, "I don't really think about that stuff much. If I do it embarrasses me. I'm embarrassed by it."

I don't know what to say to that, so I keep quiet, waiting for the rest, but there is no rest.

We talk about other stuff. My kids. His music. His new studio. How our parents are. Then I tell him that I have to go.

It's three hours earlier where he is. It's probably still light in California. I've never seen his house.

I've never seen him since he started losing his hair. It's hard to imagine what he looks like now. In the Christmas pictures each face is so small. I see him the way I saw him then, with his ripped World War II leather Air Force jacket and his guitar case and his derby hat, back when we were driving the van through Europe, carrying hash in our underpants, imagining we were reinventing the world.

I want it all. I want to approve of the person I used to be. Even her excesses—the drugs, the cigarettes, the men, the late nights, the craziness—want to believe it somehow made me what I am; not believe, as he seems to believe, that it was just an impediment, something to forget.

So which was it—triumph, exploration, some important journey, or just a big stupid mistake, a total waste of time? Was I brave or was I only stupid and selfish?

I still don't know. Did all that stuff we did just hold us back? Did it open doors for us or slam them shut?

It's easy now to see only the ridiculousness of it—the terrible clownlike costumes, the lost lives spun out and destroyed by drugs, bad driving, crazy risks.

✿

We finally stopped for one reason or another. We had a really bad trip or a friend died or we just outgrew it. And then we got on with our lives, but we always had a stash in our top drawers under our socks and once in a while we'd still get stoned with our friends and once in a while, when we came upon someone who was sort of like us—some woman with shaggy hair, some guy who had a certain look about him, we might compare nostalgic notes—how wild we were—and we felt proud that we weren't just sheep. That we weren't straight, but daring and wild and trying stuff out when all the rest of them were just trooping wearily into the fold. And then it seems as if that history makes our lives more important.

No matter how straight we've gotten, we still have this secret identity, this throwback soul.

I hate drugs now. I hate getting high. I want to be clear and clean. I have a pedometer; I walk every day. I'm in pretty good shape for somebody who's fifty. I watch what I eat. I have wine with dinner but I never have more than two glasses on special occasions. I do yoga or I work out at a gym or I do Tai Chi or some damn thing and I have an annual pap smear and a mammogram and I solemnly promise the stern nurse in her pink smock yes I do my self-examination and I actually have sometimes but now I'll *really* do it. Now I'll do it every single month. I go to the dentist twice a year. I've had some gum work done. I floss, I use a Sonicare. I dye my hair. I don't get too much sun. I wear a hat, use #30 sunscreen. I wear gloves in the garden. I need glasses now. Take Tums for calcium. Lift weights. I'm careful with myself because suddenly I understand how fragile we all are. Our parents, if they're living, they are fragile. Our children, fragile, fragile. The world a fragile, dismal, precious kind of place.

Sometimes I wish I'd done things differently, but I know I can't change that so I soldier on.

Why did I do that stuff anyway? Was it because it seemed like fun?

Getting high isn't really fun. If you break it down into the parts that make it up. Feeling sort of dizzy and off balance. Not being able to function. Feeling maybe a little sick to your stomach or having a really dry mouth or that itchy feeling like the waistband of your pants doesn't fit you right or being scared suddenly and surrounded by scary things or feeling like everybody's watching you or feeling frightened of your own face in the mirror. The kinds of things that are described as *unpleasant side effects* were what we went for. Those things weren't really fun, were they? But then they passed for fun.

On a summer day I drive into Bar Harbor to get some groceries at the Shop 'N Save. This was a mistake. The roads are clogged with cars. What was I even thinking? It's July. Everything's open and the sidewalks are full of people eating ice cream. On the village green there are kids sitting in the grass. Somebody's playing a guitar. Somebody's throwing a Frisbee. Somebody's dog with a red bandana around his neck. They dress the way we used to dress. That mixture of utility and frivolity—a lacey peasant blouse and Carhart overalls.

Further down the road, at the corner of Cottage and Main, there are three or four kids sitting on the bench. These are the colder children. I recognize one I've heard is deep into heroin. That he sells it. Some of the younger kids have a glad, alert look like they're lucky to be sitting there. The rest are dull-eyed. I find myself checking them out. They're the ones I would have felt aligned with at one time. I would have been thinking which one I wanted to sleep with. Which one to get high with. Which one not even to bother with. Now they are the dangerous ones, the sad ones, the ones we talk about in our weary community meetings: the alcohol problem, the drug problem, what to do with the Youth.

Why do they get like that?

And we wring out hands and we make up rules and we discuss and discuss and discuss and we ask our children what are you looking for? What do you want? But really, some of us know. Some of us, if we're willing to, can remember, what it was like, back in those days of our own adolescence, when the world seemed lit by a certain light. When there seemed to be something just there beyond where we stood.

They're not going to tell us. We have to figure it out for ourselves; to go back into our own lives and plunge our hands deep into our own wild histories. We have to admit to being who we were, to wanting what we wanted.

We have to remember what it was like when we were fifteen.

I

fARM BOY

THE MARYLAND COUNTRYSIDE in late fall was gray and brown like my scarf. Wet branch brown. Gray leaden sky. Abandoned fields. I sat in the hard little backseat of our yellow VW bug, bored and stupefied in my parents' car. Driven out here to the wilds of nothingness, out to a dreary afternoon with my parents' dreary friends somewhere in farthest Maryland, when I could have been up in my room listening to *The Mothers of Invention* on my stereo; drawing twisty pictures with my ink pen. Swirly letters. Bulging op art checkerboards. Enormous eyeballs. Vines. Could have gone somewhere with Cassie. Could have gone to Georgetown; done something interesting. Not this.

"It's down that lane, I think," my mother said, and we turned down a lumpy dirt driveway with fields spreading out on either side, a couple of cows, a far fence and ahead a house and barn that looked like a farm in Ohio or someplace. The country.

I pretended I was being taken to a prison in wartime. The sky seemed warlike, the cold air desolate and strange. My parents were the guards, taking me to a distant farmhouse where I would be hidden in a cellar made of dirt.

"Richard! Helen! Hi!"

A big dog bounded toward the car and a woman with long gray hair and a big sweater. A man behind her with a hand outstretched.

"Oh! And you brought Martha!"

I didn't want to get out of the car.

The big dog was straining to get at me. I was afraid of dogs. Their wet mouths. Their big teeth. Their black gums! Always leaping up and barking.

"Martha!"

My mother turned back and saw me still sitting in the backseat. She was afraid of dogs, too. Once we had held hands tightly as we passed by the fenced yard of a barking pair. What were dogs anyway? Wolves with names.

But now only, "Come on, Martha, he won't hurt you."

I got out.

She was right; he didn't hurt me, but came pressing close to me with his big wet face and his odd, irregular, canine eyes. He got as close as he could, trying to put his big black nose between my legs. I backed against the car.

"Come on!" they called to me, starting toward the house, oblivious.

I pushed the dog away from me. He was so strong. I could feel his thick, muscley shoulders through his fur. I could be pinned there forever, pressed against the side of our yellow Volkswagen while my parents and the Bragdons went away, chattering and laughing, up to the farmhouse door forgetting all about me. But then suddenly the dog stopped resisting, trotted off.

We were almost to the house when I saw another person slip out onto the porch and stand there. *They have a boy about your age.*

He was wearing jeans and a leather vest, long hair and sideburns.

"Hi," he said when we got closer.

"Jon, this is Mr. and Mrs. Dudman, and this is Martha. Maybe you can show her around. We'll have lunch in about an hour."

"Want to see my room?" he asked me and started up the stairs.

I shrugged and went after him. The house was big and bare. Wood floors and not much furniture. I followed Jon up the stairs. The voices of our parents chattered on below.

The last thing I heard was my mother saying, "I hope they get along," and Mrs. Bragdon answering, "I'm sure they will."

"Up here," Jon told me over his shoulder.

We went down a narrow hallway and up more stairs to the third floor.

"That part's the attic," he said, gesturing at a small, closed door. "You want to see it?"

"Is it scary?"

He looked at me, but it didn't matter. I didn't care if he thought it was a dumb remark. I didn't know him. He wasn't going to turn up later. He didn't live in my neighborhood. He didn't go to the same parties. He didn't hang out in Georgetown. He lived way out here. I'd never even seen him before. I probably wouldn't ever see him again. So it didn't matter. I could act any way I wanted to act. Just say whatever popped into my head.

"Scary?" he asked me.

"Yeah. You know."

"A little," he said.

That's when I knew I could like him.

The door creaked as he swung it open. Dusty light fell across a slanty space full of old boxes and tall clothes bags hanging down. I came up behind him and we stood in the doorway looking in. It was cold in there, and dim.

"I don't want to go in," I told him.

He backed out, bumping into me, and then he shut the door and latched it.

"I'll show you my room," he said.

🌀

His room was long and bright with tall windows. It was up above the branches of the fall trees, and you could see a long way across the fields.

There was a narrow bed covered with an Indian bed-spread, one broad wooden table and a shelf of books. A record player on the floor. A candle stuck in a bottle. It felt, because of the wideness of the fields below, like a lonely room up here in this far off farmhouse. A lonely room, not a normal regular teenage boy room.

"It's nice," I said.

"Yeah," he kind of looked around. "It's okay. We've only lived here a few months. We used to just come here in the summer, but my dad's working on a book, so now we're living out here."

"Where did you live before?"

"In Baltimore."

I nodded.

"Where do you go to school?"

"Lanham. Where do you go?"

"Madeira."

"Ah."

"Don't say *Ah* like you know all about me now," I told him. "Like *oh yeah she goes to this preppy girls' school.* I just go there because my parents make me."

He looked at me.

"Okay," he said. "Want to get high?"

He was checking to see if I was cool.

"Up here?" I asked him.

"Sure. I do it all the time."

"Don't your parents smell it?"

"I blow it out the window," he said. "I burn some incense. They can't tell the difference."

"But we have to eat with them." I'd only smoked pot two times before in my life.

"Look, it's not that good," he told me. "Just some hash. But if you don't want to . . ."

"No," I said. "But let's wait until after lunch and go outside and do it."

"Okay," he said.

"Here's what I do," he told me. "Want to see?"

He pushed his record player into the middle of the room. Then he put his lamp on the turntable, and he took a basket and emptied all the stuff out and put the basket over the lamp. Then he went around the room pulling down the blinds on all the windows. There were no curtains, just those dark green window shades that you see in old houses. The bright room got dim. He turned on the record player and the turntable started going around and the light shining through the basket made a design that went around and around like shadowy lace on the walls and ceiling of this boy's room.

We were silent. I sat down on the bed and he sat down beside me.

"It's sort of like a light show," he told me. "I do this sometimes when I'm here. It's better when you're stoned."

It was nice and I wished it were even nicer, but it also felt sad that this was what he did—sat in his high-up third-floor room with all his brothers and sisters grown up and gone away and looked at the light shining through a basket going around and around on his walls.

We heard somebody yelling from downstairs.

"It's my dad," Jon said. "I think it's time for lunch."

✿

I was glad we weren't stoned. It would have been too weird. It was already weird enough. Jon's parents were the kind of people who tried to talk to you as if they already knew you. As if they were your age, or you theirs. Jon seemed okay with this, but it made me nervous. He called my parents *Helen* and

Dick and didn't seem to notice that my mother was a little taken aback. Later she'd say something about it.

The food was good, but I was embarrassed eating in front of Jon, who kept looking at me across the table. I just ate a little. Nobody said anything. They'd put the dog in the kitchen. I could hear him shuffling around in there and his snickery nails clattering against the door as he tried to get out.

"What are you going to do after lunch?" Jon's mother asked him.

"I'm going to take Martha out and show her around. The barn. The field. The creek," he answered.

She nodded. "Good idea. We just have cookies for dessert. Why don't you take some with you?"

The dog came along but it was okay, he just ran off across the fields like any dog would run, not paying attention to us, which was fine with me.

Jon started off across the fields and I followed. We came to a bunch of trees beside a narrow creek.

"It freezes over," he told me. "It's really cool. You can see the leaves underneath. They look great. All brown and flat. Kind of like a painting."

He'd taken a pipe out of a little suede pouch and a chunk of dark brown hash wrapped in tin foil. I'd never seen hash before. It looked like a piece of crayon.

We came in close to the creek where the tall tree trunks rose up around us and made a shadowy place.

The water was clear and looked cold and glittery. We stood close together over the pipe as he lit it and sucked in the pale smoke, handed it to me.

I took a deep toke and it made me cough and gusts of smoke came out of my mouth.

"Easy," he said, and held the pipe while I coughed and coughed. Tears came to my eyes. "Here, try again."

It was kind, the way he said it, and it didn't make me feel stupid the way I might have felt if someone else had said it in a different way.

I took another toke, not so deep this time, and it was all right.

We took turns and each time the hash glowed bright orange like a little coal in the bowl of the blue pipe.

I was getting high. I could start to feel it. It was different than the times I'd tried pot. Clearer. Higher. Less fuzzy.

"This is great," I said, and even my voice sounded clear and high and perfect.

He smiled at me and now he seemed familiar.

"I love to get high," he told me. "Love it. I have to watch that I don't do it all the time."

That seemed romantic to me, and ruined.

"What do you do out here when you're stoned?" I asked him.

It seemed like a funny question, and I almost started laughing, but he took it seriously, staring out through the trees.

"I come down here," he told me. "I write things. Poetry. I draw. When we get back, I'll show you my drawings."

Then I knew he was someone I was going to know after all. He wrote poetry. He was going to show me his drawings. We were connected in some way.

We smoked a little more and then he tipped the last of the coal into the damp, cold earth and stamped it out.

"Can't have a fire," he told me. He was a woodsman! He was a farm boy! He knew these nature things!

We walked along the creek until we came to a big gray barn.

"Can I climb up in the hayloft?" I asked him.

"Sure."

It reminded me of the barn in Maine where my sister and I used to go on foggy days when we were kids. We'd climb the wooden ladder up to the hayloft and slide down into the piled hay below. We'd swing on a rope hung from a rafter. It had felt elemental. It had felt like I was having an actual childhood like the kids in books. Not the made-up pseudo childhood of Washington, D.C., but a sort of E. B. Whitish, Laura Ingalls Wilder, crayon drawing of a childhood.

This barn had that same smell—that mysterious smell of animal and hay. That deep earth smell.

I felt graceful in my cowboy boots and tight jeans. I felt tall and thin. I grabbed the strong wooden rungs of the ladder, hoisted myself up.

"Be careful," Jon said, and I liked that; like I was daring.

She's crazy, he might tell his parents later, shaking his head back and forth like a puzzled dog.

She's nuts, he might say later in his room, while the basket light on the turntable went around and around. But he would be saying it in an admiring way, remembering my odd grace as I clambered nimbly up the ladder to the high loft and stood above him, looking down.

"Is there a swing?"

"No, I don't think so. There used to be, but I don't know. It's gone."

"Oh."

I stood a little longer looking around the big dark barn, breathing in the smell of the place. Wanting to stay up there. Wanting him to come up there with me. Wanting something. I didn't know what yet. Something. But instead I came down, sliding down into the hay the way we used to in Maine.

"We had such a nice time."

My mother put out her hands and gave Mrs. Bragdon a hug. "What a place you've got here!"

"Wonderful to see you."

"Let me know about the book. If I can help you," my father said.

Jon and I stood together by the car. We weren't as stoned now. We'd walked all over across the muddy fields, broken cornstalks and the wide-open pastures.

I felt good, outdoorsy, competent, and tired.

"So maybe I'll see you when I come into the city," he said.

"Okay," I answered. Now I had to go back, chained to my parents, returned to the dark cubicle of the backseat.

He looked away from me. I wanted him to say something else, but that was all.

Maybe it was my turn, but I didn't know what to say either.

2

THE PARTY AT THE
MAYFLOWER HOTEL

THERE WAS GOING to be a party in December.

It wasn't exactly a coming-out party, but it was going to be really fancy and at the Mayflower Hotel downtown. There was going to be dancing, and you had to wear a long dress. All my friends from Madeira were going to be there—the ones who rode the bus with me from Georgetown out into the country every day—Cassie and Sydney Jane, beautiful Dianna, Eleanor, and the rest. Some of the Boarders were invited too. They would be spending the night at the homes of some of the Day Girls—the ones with the biggest houses and the wrought-iron fences and the wrought-iron mothers with their blonde coifs and tiny pink wool suits—the women of Washington who had dinner parties with fancy china and names on little cards and famous husbands.

My mother and I went shopping way out in the country near Alexandria. Beyond the far, muddy fields there were outcroppings of tiny, elegant stores. "I know a place we can get a dress," she'd told me.

We didn't spend much time together anymore. We used to go to Best & Company on Wisconsin Avenue for the white dress with the pink sash. The navy coat with brass buttons—my sister Annie had one, too—the Mary Janes.

"We'll go out to lunch," my mother told me.

It was all right to be with her because it was so far out of town. We weren't going to run into anybody I knew. And it was Saturday, so she had a day off. She wouldn't be going to the office in her work clothes and mascara, coming back all tired, and sitting on the couch with the eagle slipcover, *what is it, honey?* with her exhausted face.

The shop was carpeted; we made no sound. Everything in the whole place was white.

The store lady was infinitesimal and exquisite. She wore a wide, patent leather belt and her hair was some other substance. It was blonde and hard like a big piece of hard, shiny candy.

"Certainly," she kept saying, as if she didn't notice my raggedy hair, my blue jeans, cowboy boots, my army jacket, and, "of course."

There were hardly any clothes in there. Not racks and racks like Woodward & Lothrup. Most of the dresses were poufy and girly, but there was one dress that stood out from all the white foam dreams. It was tall and narrow and it had green and pink swirly shapes twisting into other shapes. It looked magic. It was *psychedelic*.

The dressing room was flouncy and white and pretty as a wedding. When I put on the dress I looked beautiful. I looked like a beautiful teenage girl with my flushed face. Breasts. Hips.

I came out of the dressing room wearing the dress.

"Oh yes!" my mother said, holding her coat in her arms. Standing the way she stood, with her feet sticking out to the sides. Looking at me as if I'd done something wonderful.

The woman with the tiny waist cocked her head to one side.

"Oh I think this will do! And a little color? I think pink." She touched one silvery finger to my shoulder, "Just that color, a little lipstick to pick up the pink, to bring it all together. Don't you think?

"Oh, Helen!" she said in a kind, sisterly voice, "she's going to be beautiful!"

How did she know my mother's name? My mother had secrets from me.

I went back into the dressing room. Pulled on my own clothes that now felt tight and unfamiliar. I wanted to be the pretty girl I'd seen in the three mirrors—one on each side and one facing forward so that in my pink and my green, my dream of a dress, I had gone on and on.

♠

At Lord & Taylor in the Bird Cage Restaurant we sat in white metal chairs and had chicken salad sandwiches and lemonade. Coconut cake for dessert. The dress, in a long white dress bag, lay spread out in the backseat of the car.

"And you'll need shoes," our fairy saleslady had warned us. "Get white ones, and have them dyed to match."

I had no idea about all this. Shoes you could dye. Little stores with only a handful of dresses.

My mother knew about this stuff. It must have come with her jobs. She had changed when I wasn't looking. She had gotten fancy.

She was still my own mother with the khaki skirt. With the blue checked shirtwaist sitting on the front porch reading a letter from my father who was away in Vietnam. With her wuzzy hair and her glasses and her vacuum cleaner and her big brown coat in winter when she used to pull us on the sled. But now she was also this.

✧

On the night of the party we drove through the transformed, lit-up streets of Washington to the house full of round tables for the dinner. It was so embarrassing! We clotted in the upstairs hallway, stuffed ourselves into the bathroom, looked at our faces, at our breasts, at our new dresses, our behinds—did they look too big? Everybody's hair had to be fixed and then fixed again. We were all exquisite.

Then the cars again to the Mayflower Hotel in downtown nighttime Washington through the streams of lights and traffic.

The hotel was plush, with big red chairs and chandeliers in the lobby. The party was upstairs.

Then the bathroom again with its tufted pink silk

benches and the Black lady in the gray uniform who sat
beside the little dish of dimes dispensing fresh white towels
from a basket. I didn't have any change to give her. I didn't
want to look at her. She didn't look at me. She looked as
though her feet hurt and she had to sit there with her hurting
feet while all of us, the white girls in our bright dresses,
whirled and stooped before the mirror. There was a certain
way you did it; bending your knees and leaning slightly back
to touch your hair like you were doing the limbo.

We fussed with our hair at the mirror and then we all
spilled out again into the hallway and down to the big room
with the long, mirrored wall and rows of rose-colored chairs
and grinning chaperones and other grown-ups that we didn't
know, somebody's parents, and the music playing and all the
boys in their tuxedos.

"Look, over there! John Kenton and Paul Wright!"

Sydney Jane dipped her head to whisper to me. Where
had she learned to do that? Like my mother, she had new
tricks that she'd learned somewhere. I was astounded by her
grown-up ways. Didn't we all just duck our heads and giggle? Some did, but, it turned out, we did not.

"Which ones?"

"You see those two guys, over by the door? Who look like
they're up to something?"

I did. I'd heard about them.

John was bad and handsome, blond and dangerous. I'd
heard the girls talking about him in the locker room. How he'd
do anything. They said his name and giggled. I would have
recognized him, even if Sydney Jane hadn't pointed him out.

"God, he's gorgeous," she said.

I would have recognized his type anywhere. They were the ones who got the girl but didn't even want her. Sat with their arm around her and their eyes far off. A blond Rhett Butler. Who drove too fast, who drank too much, got kicked out of school, did drugs and didn't care.

His companion, Paul, was the kind for me. He seemed a little bit mysterious and sad. He was the one with the brown hair. Brown eyes. Second in command. The one who stood a little apart. The one you talked to. The one who knew the worst about the star and loved him anyway.

"What's Paul like?" I asked Sydney Jane.

"I think he's nice. His dad's with the CIA," she said, but she wasn't really paying attention; she was looking at John. She was fixed upon him. "I don't really know much about him. They're friends, I think."

That was the one. And this was the night, so it didn't surprise me when the two of them sauntered toward us as the music swelled again and the other invisible couples began to dance.

John bowed to Sydney Jane. "May I?" he asked in this ironic way, and we all knew what he was really asking.

Paul looked into my eyes. He was a little taller than I was, not much. His eyes were different than I had expected. Not brown at all, but pale green-gray.

Then I was dancing with him. Me! With Paul Wright, the secret agent's son, on the slippery dance floor upstairs at the Mayflower Hotel!

We danced for hours. Fast dances. Slower dances. Slower still.

He got me punch to drink. It looked old-fashioned, the way he balanced two cut-glass cups in one hand, weaving his way back to me across the room.

I felt as if I were in *The Great Gatsby.* Everything so fancy and unreal.

The way I talked. How I could joke with him. And dip my head. And look across the room and see Sydney Jane dipping her head too in that same way to hear what John was saying. It was an instinct—how to dip your head!

It was almost too much—the music and the way Paul held me as the music slowed. He pressed against me and I could feel him against me and what I thought must be his penis or maybe it was just his hipbone pushing against me as we were pressed so close. His hot breath on my neck. His firm hands around me. I glanced up as we drifted through the room and saw in the sparkling mirror the sparkling girl I was. I almost didn't recognize myself. The pretty hair, the pretty flushed face, the dreamy smile. The beautiful and psychedelic dress.

"I'd like to see you," Paul said in my ear.

"Mmmmm hmmmm," I murmured in my dreamy way.

The evening could go on like this forever. A confusion of desire and false promises and drifting, lovely girls.

❧

"I think he really likes you," Sydney Jane told me in the bathroom.

The Black attendant stared ahead, towels at the ready. Black swollen ankles crossed, her too-tight dress.

I stared into the mirror.

Around us the other girls all buzzed and fizzed. I saw the two of us. I saw myself. How pretty I looked. How magical and special.

"How about you? How about John?" I asked her.

She laughed a tinkly laugh. "Oh he's a bad boy," she told me. "Oh he's wicked!"

She knew more than I did. She wanted more.

I wanted only this—the drift and glaze and glimmer of the dance. The press and stumble of our slow procession.

"It's almost over," I told Sydney Jane. "Let's go back in."

We wove our way through throngs of disappointed people. The boys who hadn't found a partner and pretended not to care, bunched in the hallway with their acne and their gawkiness and covert glances. The fat girls in the chairs making their spiteful remarks. I heard them hush as I walked by and then from one of them, "Did you see her dancing? How close they were?"

"He was practically jerking off on her," I heard.

Was that it? But I didn't care. In fact, it made me feel proud and daring.

He could do anything to me. He could do anything at all with me, that night.

"You're back," he told me, and he pulled me close.

But then the night was over and I scribbled my name and number on a napkin. Sydney Jane and I were being picked up by my father. And when we got down to the crowded sidewalk to wait for him, the boys were gone.

✿

"Did you hear from him?" she asked me Monday morning.

"No," I said, trying not to show the way I felt. "Did you?"

"John came by yesterday," she said. "We took a walk."

The way she said it I knew that there was more, but then Mr. Finney our history teacher was standing there implacable and boring in his brown tweed jacket and it was time to stop talking and pretend to listen.

❧

After classes, during that dull, darkening dip before the bus left at four-thirty, we were supposed to *get acquainted* with the boarders or *participate in activities* or we could study. Some girls did. You'd see them hunched over their books and papers in the library at the long tables, heads bent attentively as children at their work.

Sydney Jane and I walked slowly across the damp December campus with our books pressed up against our chests, up into the woods on the gravel track that led to a high bluff over the swirling beige Potomac far below.

She told me bits and pieces about her afternoon with John.

That's how she always told things. One piece and then another piece, like she was showing me photographs of the sides of things—somebody's elbow, a hand holding a glass, a piece of a shoulder with the head turned away. So I'd just ask her in my straight-out way, *So did you do it?* and then she'd laugh that laugh of hers and say, *Oh, Martha!*

I think they did do it, or almost did it, that day after the dance. I know they smoked some grass together on the roof of the apartment house near where she lived. You could go up there and look out beyond a sea of trees in wintertime; the billowing gray waves and their dark branches spidery and fingery against the sky.

They must have huddled together on the roof, leaned against the lip of the ledge. He must have put his arm around her, so they could feel each other's bodies; she small and birdlike in her jacket with her hair fine as a baby's hair against his face; he taller, more substantial beneath his coat, his arms around her strong and hard and young, his face bent down to hers.

How it must have been. Different than the times I'd fumbled through with other boys.

It wouldn't be anything like that with these guys. They knew what they were doing.

You could tell John knew, the way he looked, that cocky look of his, that careless way he flipped his blond hair back. His WASP rights to girls. Those St. Albans boys were all like that—like blond and haughty princes with their perfect pointy profiles and careless ways.

Sydney Jane always knew much more than she let on.

"So then what?"

She just laughed. "Oh I don't know. He's got a million girls."

But didn't that bother her? Didn't that make her almost crazy? Him with his girls? Him with his million girls? Didn't that make her mad? Make her want to call him up and see if his line was busy? See if he answered the phone, and then hang up not speaking? Didn't that make her want to drive her mother's car again and again past his house in the darkness with the lights off trying to see in the windows?

Didn't any one thing play over and over in her mind the way I played the same shows over and over in my mind: *if I'd only, if I'd maybe, why didn't I think of, how could I have*—didn't she do that too?

♦

"You think too much," Cassie told me on the bus ride home.

"You worry about too much," she said.

Well, she could talk, she was from California. In California nobody thought. Ever. People just walked around in bikinis in the sun, flipped their hair back, sang songs on the beach, played volleyball, went surfing. It wasn't real life. Not like the East Coast where we darker ones lived all bunched up with our problems and our worries and our thinking thinking thinking. Which felt right.

I couldn't *not* think. I couldn't *not* worry. Because most of the time there was no peace for me. There was no quiet. There were always a million things poking into me. Pricking at me with their prickly presence. Poking at me with their pointy elbows.

What did she mean and *why did I say* and *how did he know* and *did he think* and *did they like me* and *was it good enough* and everything.

It was like I was always awake in the darkness staring into the dark room full of worries that I couldn't fix.

You're too sensitive, the girl on the playground in the fourth grade with her self-satisfied hairdo and her saddle shoes.

My eyes filled up with tears.

You shouldn't worry so much.

Don't think about it—my dance teacher—*just let go! Dance!*

But how could I let go? How could I float away? How could I ever? I wanted to, but I was dark and twisty in my own dark places.

Out on the lawn I might see them—the other girls of the world in their white dresses. Floaty sashes. Dashing off across the wide, dark grass. In California. Oklahoma. In my dreams. But I was always there with me. Always too much there. Observing, taking note, reminding, blinding, tapping myself on the shoulder. Remember this, remember that. I couldn't ever just *be.*

3

MAYBE I'M A LESBIAN

BUT THEN JON CALLED. He had to get off the farm, he said. He was coming on Saturday. My mother said he could spend the night on the living room couch. We were going to a movie at the Circle Theatre on M Street.

"Do you mind foreign films with subtitles?" he had asked me over the phone.

My sister Annie was gone for the weekend. My parents were out. I was all alone in the house when Jon came. It was already getting dark.

He looked the same but different with his long hair and his leather vest. He stood there on the porch before me and I wondered if he was going to turn out to be the person who changed my life. Who finally understood everything about me. If I was going to have to like that vest.

We walked up Newark Street past Rosedale, the old estate

in the next block that was mysterious and dark and bunchy with its bunchy boxwoods in the night. I wanted to tell him how I used to play there when I was a kid. How we'd climb down into the enormous boxwoods, and how their twisty branches were like magic caves where we used to act out stories full of witches and elves. But I didn't say anything. It might come out wrong, sound dumb, and I felt so perfect, walking beside him toward the bright lights of Wisconsin Avenue.

✿

It wasn't a foreign movie after all. It was *A Thousand Clowns* with Jason Robards. I'd seen it before; I loved that movie. That's what I was going to do: live in a messy, arty apartment in Manhattan. Let my son choose his own name. Have an Oriental screen with dragons painted on it and sing old songs *yes sir, that's my baby* and ride bicycles around New York in black and white and be in love.

When we came out of the movie it had rained, and we walked up M Street toward Georgetown in the shimmery night with the wet pavement and the lights shining off the puddles. There was a tree with little drops of water all over it that glinted in the night. We stopped and stared upward and we weren't even stoned. We weren't even holding hands but I knew it meant something. The night, the movie, this one tree.

"It's beautiful, isn't it?" I asked him.

He was silent beside me. We didn't touch.

The tree was glistening. The leaves looked silver.

And then it started to rain and we ran for the bus stop and huddled under the awning at Woolworth's waiting for the bus to take us home.

By the time we got to Newark Street the rain had stopped, but we ran down the road anyway, breathless and excited in the black night. Rosedale was strange and empty beside us—the far-off house high up on the hill, unlit behind the magnolia trees with their big branches and hard, oval leaves.

My parents were home now, and they were still up.

"I brought a sleeping bag down for Jon. He can sleep on the green couch," my father said.

The house seemed small and unprivate. The kitchen leading right into the dining room. The dining room into the hall, which was next to the living room. Upstairs my room, my parents' room. Side by side and stuck too close together. There was no way to keep secrets in this house.

"You want something to eat?" my mother offered.

"You want something?" I asked him.

I hoped he didn't. I didn't want him to eat anything that might require my also eating something. The two of us at the kitchen table with the lights on munching on cookies for God's sake with glasses of milk!

"Nah, I'm okay," he said.

My parents went upstairs.

Good.

When they were gone, Jon and I went into the living room and sat on the eagle couch where my mother sat in the evening with her book.

"I love that movie," I told him.

"Yeah, it's good," he said.

We sat there side by side.

I didn't know what to do, so I lit a cigarette and he asked me, "Why do you smoke?" in a pesky way.

I was surprised. Didn't he have long hair? Didn't he live in the country? Didn't he do that light thing with his basket and his record player?

"Don't you?"

"Just grass," he told me. "And hash. Not cigarettes."

Like they were something dirty.

"I don't know. I like it. I love to smoke," I told him, but I was embarrassed now, smoking.

There was a little silence.

"I guess I'm nervous," I told him.

"Why?" he asked me like he didn't really care.

"I don't know. I guess because we're sitting here and I don't know what's supposed to happen next."

This was the sort of open wound of a thing you could say to someone you were connected to. You should be able to say anything, and they would get it.

But he said only, "I don't see why. It's obvious."

I felt odd and light and nervous. I put my cigarette out. It was stupid anyway, smoking in the house. My parents hated it. They would have to pretend they believed me when I said that he was the one who had been smoking.

Still nothing happened. I could hear the silence upstairs, and the rain coming down outside the house.

We sat right across from the long couch where he was going to sleep in the sleeping bag we used to take on camping trips. There was nothing to say. I wanted to fill up the silence with stories. The story of the sleeping bag. The story of the raccoon at the campsite in Kansas. The story of the time I almost died from mosquito bites. Anything to stop it being so quiet and expectant in the room.

I could feel his arm through his sleeve touching my arm through my sleeve. The thick brown corduroy fabric. The meaty bone of his elbow. How close we sat.

And then, because he still didn't say anything, I put my hands up over my face and made a little noise. "Enh!"

"What?" he sounded annoyed.

"I don't know," I said for the thirtieth time. But what else could I say? I *didn't* know. What to do next. What to feel.

"I guess I just don't know how I feel. Sitting here, next to you."

He took this as a signal, and put his arm around my shoulder and sort of squeezed me and then, the way I'd hoped he would, he pried my fingers away from my face, and he reached up, turned off the light, and started kissing me.

🌀

His tongue was big and wet and foreign in my mouth. And his face, so near my own face, was strange and alien and he smelled weird. I tried to do whatever I was supposed to do back, sticking my own tongue into that crowded place, that wasn't my mouth anymore or his mouth, but just a vast corridor full of teeth and smooth walls and strange, slippery, soft, damp places like a cellar full of bodies or an underwater tomb.

We kissed for a really long time.

I kept my eyes shut but my mind twirled. I was in the rain. I was running down the pavement. I was tiptoeing over to the bottom of the staircase listening to hear if my parents were still awake.

He held me tightly around the shoulder with one hand and with the other he pushed and rubbed at the front of me, like someone scrubbing a window, hands spread wide, rubbing and rubbing.

After awhile he fell back against the couch; stared straight ahead. Even with the lights off I could see him.

"You're not responding," he said. "It's like you're not really here."

Where had he learned words like that? How did he know what to say?

"I know," I said humbly, dumbly. "It's how I get."

"Maybe I'm a lesbian," I added glumly.

"You think so?"

I could tell he sort of liked that.

"I don't know. I mean, I never really *have* felt anything."

"Well, there's only one thing to do then," he said, sitting there in the half dark.

He said it like of course I would know what that one thing was, but I didn't. I didn't know if he meant I should go up to bed, or that he should do something to me. What. Or I should do something with somebody else? But then *who?* And where was I supposed to get him? Jon was here. Wouldn't he do?

And all the rest of it—that connection I'd felt to him. That somehow had nothing to do with this. That part was gone. Now there was just this sour man in the dark, older and different than the boy on the farm, than the boy in the rain. He seemed angry and fed up, but then, astoundingly, he stood, took my hand, and led me down the room to the long couch, where my father liked to nap on Saturday afternoons and my mother would say, *Go in and wake him up girls, but do it gently,* and we would go in and run our fingers like feathers on our father's face or my sister would pat his shoulder gently through the afghan and say in a whispery voice intended to sound womanly, I thought resentfully, *Wake up Daddy, it's time for supper.* To that couch full of my father's dreams, Jon led me now.

I had my shoes off, and I could feel, through my tights, every nub and stubble of my mother's carpet.

This time he lay down beside me. It was very dark in this part of the room. He kissed the side of my face, licked the corner of my mouth, and slid his hands up under my dress, covering my breast with his hand which felt big and warm and hard against my skin.

He squeezed my breast and I did feel something. Something. He pinched my nipple and I made a little sound that sounded as if it were coming out of somebody else.

He put his mouth back over my mouth and this time it was different. This time there were so many different things going on at once. My nipple. His hot, hard hand on my breast. His knee pushing itself between my thighs. His hand—which hand?—some other, extra hand, pulling down my underpants and my tights so that the elastic waistband was digging into my thighs, and then his fingers poking and prodding at me and rubbing and I felt all wet.

He pulled my tights down further and there was a lot of

rummaging and confusion and then it wasn't his finger anymore. It was something else.

Oh God. It was his penis! I jerked away from him.

"What are you doing?" I whispered at him, shocked.

"I think you know," he said, his voice like an enemy. "I think you know what I'm doing."

"Well stop it!" I told him.

He yanked angrily away from me. Lay back, squeezed beside me on the narrow couch.

I was panting. I didn't know what I was. If I was furious. If I was about to cry.

"Well what did you think was going to happen?" he asked. His voice was sulky.

"I don't know," I said.

"Can we just talk?" I asked him humbly.

He made a snorting noise like a horse.

"I don't exactly feel like talking," he told me.

There was this silence.

Then I moved toward him and put my hand on the side of his face. I knew how to do this. This part. Touching him tenderly. Stroking what I liked of him—his arms, his chest. His soft hair.

I didn't want to touch his penis. Didn't want to know about it or even have it be there.

"What if my parents came down?" I asked him.

"Well, there's nothing going on *now*, is there?" he said.

We lay beside each other in a moody silence.

I couldn't tell if I was supposed to go now. Or if we could do more—the parts I liked. The things I wanted to do. The kissing part. The breast part, that was okay. Even the part where he had his finger inside me. Except for the noise it made. Like someone wearing sneakers when they'd walked in puddles. A squishing sound. But it had felt—not good exactly—but interesting. And wasn't it what you were supposed to do?

I ran my hand tentatively over his strong chest. I could feel the light swath of hair in the middle where his shirt was open. I ran my fingers down it, down to his navel, and he shivered. Shivered! Just below his navel I could feel the line continue, deepen, darken. The line of hair leading down.

I knew that just beyond the graze of my fingers there it was. His penis. The fat soft worm Mary McCarthy called it in *The Group*.

"I think you ought to go to bed," he told me.

I didn't want to. I wanted the rest of something. I wanted him to be the kind of person I had imagined he was.

I wanted him to touch me again only not in such a hurry.

I wanted to push my body against his body, to have our clothes not grabbed off, tugged down, yanked and wrinkled, but all our clothes to sort of float away off our bodies and our wonderful skin to be joined in some way that did not involve actual penetration but was satisfying and religious and sweet.

He gave a sigh, as if I had worn him out with all my thinking.

"Jon?"

"Yeah?"

"Are you mad?"

That sigh again.

"No. I'm not mad. Are you a virgin?"

I was shocked by the question. The word itself was a word

you almost didn't say, like *vagina* or *penis* or oh God *intercourse* or *nipple* or any of those things. A virgin.

"I guess so, yeah," I answered.

"You *guess* so?" he repeated in his angry way.

"Well, yeah."

As long as I didn't have to say the word it wasn't so bad.

"Why?" he asked me.

That stumped me. Why indeed? I didn't know why or why not. I didn't want to talk about these things with him. But I felt as if I had done something wrong. As if somehow, without knowing it, I had cheated him or stolen something from him. Something he was supposed to have. Or maybe it was like I'd handed it to him and then said *oh no wait, I guess I don't want you to have that after all.*

"You need to figure out what you want," he said to me.

✦

In the morning I didn't want to come down, and by the time I did, he was gone.

"He said he had to get the bus," my mother told me.

She was busy in the kitchen and didn't look at me.

"I'll air this out," my father said, coming through the bright kitchen, carrying the sleeping bag held out, away from him, as if he knew.

The rain was gone. The backyard, through the kitchen window, was bright and sunny. My father hung the sleeping bag over the clothesline and I ate the toast my mother made for me.

That was it. That was the last time I ever heard from him. I thought for a little while that he might just turn up. That I would see him again—at a movie, at a party, at a concert with a light show. He'd be standing there with red and purple splotches all over his face. *Hey* he'd say. It was the sort of thing he might like, he from his farm and his barn. But I'd never seen him before, so why would I start seeing him now?

I felt myself as if for broken bones. For a broken heart.

"Tell her I'll give her a call, next time I'm in town," he'd told my mother.

But he didn't call.

Was I supposed to call him?

I didn't think so.

Maybe there was something I should have done. I needed to figure it out for the next time. Should I have done more? Done less? Was it because I let him do those things or because I didn't let him do everything he wanted? Was he right, that thing he'd whispered in the dark to me, that I wasn't a lesbian, I was a Puritan? A *Puritan?* Wasn't that like a Pilgrim or something with a big hat and a gigantic collar with big bright ugly buckles on their shoes? Just because I didn't want him sticking his strong weird wiry penis into me did that mean that I was—*frigid?* Had he said that, too?

In the locker room at school I heard Suki Barber tell another girl, "I can't help it. I'm a nympho. Let's face it. I'm a slut."

She looked like a slut, I thought, with her loose, floppy mouth and her flat, hanging-down hair.

Her breasts were slut breasts.

I wanted that mark of reckless gaiety to be mine. Not *slut* exactly, but something more daring, more darling than the words he'd named me with: *Puritan, frigid.* Even *lesbian* sounded more interesting and artistic.

Not just Martha.

It hung on: that feeling of breathlessness and wriggling embarrassment and all the questions and wishing I could talk to him, just talk to him, just ask him *why?* What should I have done instead? But then that passed over, and I felt hopeless. It would be winter soon and here I was. I'd be sixteen in January. I didn't even know a single thing.

4

S E X

PAUL DIDN'T CALL.

Jon didn't call.

Winter wore on. The snow came; the thin, wet, disappointing snow of Washington. The skies remained gray, leaden.

In mid-February, in the dull heart of winter, we stood at the Georgetown bus stop in clumps with our books and our purses waiting for the bus.

There was nothing but the bus and the rain and the disappointing snow and the dull classrooms and the sound of Mr. Hobson's dull voice droning Latin conjugations and his sarcastic sharp comment, *Maybe* you'd *like to lead the class, Martha?* And his pompous belly pressing out his pompous professorial jacket, but we knew he wasn't any kind of fancy tweed professor but a tiresome loser with his Latin book tucked up high under his arm as he strode the campus manfully dressed in his corduroy pants, his tweed jacket, his open-necked shirt—a parody of himself—a pipe in his pocket. *Loser* written all over him.

And Mr. Angleton, the thin art teacher with the English accent and the longish brown hair and the kind, distant eyes behind his glasses. He was so thin and with the accent that we wondered if he might be homosexual. Or might be available and have affairs. Or might be dull and married. He was so thin he was almost transparent as he leaned over our drawings.

He hardly had a body at all beneath his clothes, no ass to speak of; did he even have any of that cumbersome equipment we knew men had? Knew from the brothers and the fathers we had glimpsed, knew from the bad boys who pressed their thick plump penises against us at the dances! At parties outside, leaning against a wall, on couches, in the hallway, anywhere, all of them—they all seemed stuffed into their pants and full of testosterone and thick, hoarse-voiced excitement—but what about him? Mr. Angleton? Did he have one? Or just the vacant sameness like a boy doll with plastic limbs and then a smooth, faint lump—was he a Ken doll underneath those baggy arty English pants of his?

There were no boys in our school. There was only the weary sameness of girls. The fat girls, tall girls, tiny girls, thin girls, with their straight or curly hair. Their faces pale and set with winter's desperation. Their disappointing, flattish breasts under the sweaters of their uniforms. Pale winter thighs. Their battered hockey knees, their chapped hands, lank strides, dull, high chatter and their yellow teeth.

❖

But boys.

If we liked them, we said they were cute, like the short, cute one in junior high school that all the girls liked until seventh grade when his face exploded in pimples—red lumps and big oozy pus-filled white things. Craters and volcanoes. His face all swollen where once it had been lean and foxlike, *cute.*

❖

He's cute, we'd say. Cuddly.

When we were younger, twelve or thirteen, we read teen magazines, ashamed of ourselves, Jenny Truesdale and I; walked to the drugstore a few blocks away from her Arlington home, where nobody *thank God* would know me although she might have to go back there someday with her mother getting a prescription, with her father getting Band-Aids or a spiral notebook and they'd recognize her, everybody pointing: *she's the one.*

The one who, with her giggling, hot-faced friend bought *Sixteen Magazine. Top Forty.* Bought *Teen Scene. Tiger Beat.* It was so embarrassing! We giggled blindly over the racks of magazines, the cartoon flowers meant to be psychedelic—the mod teen scene, Swinging London Mop Top Pop Scene—the flower power pix with hot stars fotos inside—Herman's Hermits. Chad & Jeremy. Fat old Elvis—who even liked him anymore? Some middle-aged gambling losers in Las Vegas. But Peter & Gordon. The wicked, sexy, and disheveled Stones. Of course the Beatles.

We sat under Jenny's parents' dining room table with the record player playing over and over, Peter Noone singing *Why does the sun go on shining? Why do these eyes of mine see? Don't they know it's the end of the world, when you don't love me anymore?* Oooooohhhhh. And making ourselves cry, actually bringing tears to our eyes. *Oh that's so sad. That's so sweet!*

Even though it was cheesy, we entered the contests with our own names because what if we did win the trip to London to sit in on a recording session? A boat trip in California with Jan & Dean? To meet the Beach Boys! Even Gene Pitney. My sister liked the gravelly way he sang "A Town Without Pity" standing all alone in a black shirt on *Shindig*.

The cute boys were cuddly as monkeys with their floppy hairdos and with funny, sticking-out teeth. We knew they were nice boys. They would smile their crooked smiles and wrap their sweet arms around us and life with them would be *sunshine lollipops and rainbows everything that's wonderful is what* we'd feel when we were together—*brighter than a lucky penny when they were near* etc. but would they want *us*? We weren't cute. We were too big, too fat or too thin, not all bubbly and bouncy like the girls they sang about with their long straight shiny go go hair and their bright eyes and rosy cheeks and little short flirty skirts and their pom poms. We were flat-chested, too big-breasted, big-assed, thick-lipped, frizzy-haired, long-faced, squinty-eyed, acne-scarred, large-nosed, Jewish mongrel losers.

How could we compete with the girlfriends that they already had in London and in California in their itsy bitsy bikinis with their tans and perfect bright-toothed smiles and their bouncing big blond effortless hair?

Or even Twiggy with her long legs and knees that stuck out bony and adorable like a little girl's and thighs that weren't like our thighs, like the thighs we knew, but straight and lean as arms! Oh God! How could we?

They were so cute, the cute boys, and we wanted them with the one part of ourselves that still loved cuddly, dear things: stuffed animals and mommy's house; but then there were the darker ones who moved us in a different way.

Mick Jagger with his thick, dangerous lips and raggedy hair.

Jeans slung low and tight and not innocently loose like the cute ones or in a little uniform with a Nehru jacket like the Beatles, but dangerous and sneering. He wouldn't be all croony bubblegum and teeny bop, but would move in on you with a smile that was like that scary smile alone in the house, the one in the living room waiting. Smile of danger and death. Sinister, sexy smile.

That, too.

The boys we were likely to meet would be mostly like the first kind. Cute. We wanted the mean ones and we were afraid of them.

Sex was a mystery we didn't get. We knew the words but didn't know what they stood for. *Balls* for example. Which you couldn't say, starting in about fifth grade, because it was funny and made the boys laugh and even some of the girls but why? Something to do with penises but we weren't sure. Then all those rhyming words like *dick* and *prick* and even *stick* and *fairy,* which used to mean gossamer wings, were off limits and there were all those other rude words, crude words: *boob* and *tit* and *cock* and *cunt* and *cum* and *suck* and *fuck* and *sixty-nine*. Even the numbers! God! They got those too!

And what exactly was it? In that bulge? In the bulge in the tight wheat-colored pants of the tall boy Nick Tortel who had liked Bambi Walker in the eighth grade, who bounced down the hall with his books under one long arm, who flipped his hair back in a certain way which meant that he was cool and first in command not like his little errand boy his henchman Max Shapiro who trotted along beside him, shorter, darker, quieter but with his own bulge too. They had them, all of them had them, even the geeky nerdy boy Roger Fairweather with the glasses and the big round face who embarrassed me by holding the door open for me with a big pumpkin grin on his big round stupid acne face as if I could like him, as if I'd deign! He had his own bulge, too.

But what was it exactly? You knew or you didn't know. You'd say or you'd say you'd say but you didn't say because you either knew and didn't say or you didn't know and couldn't say and I sure didn't know. I couldn't say.

Something.

A penis. I knew that much from Personal and Family Living when we all squirmed at our seats in the hot class thinking *oh God now they know I know they've got one. Oh God and vagiiiiiina. Now they know I've got one of those, too. Oh God how embarrassing! Oh God!* and giggled helplessly in the face of it all because what else was there to do?

A penis. It was a long thing like a hot dog but I thought maybe with some kind of ridges on it. Kind of like a Slinky. I'd seen a few of them, of course. Like the time Eddie Tinker showed me his under the ping pong table before his dad came down red-faced and furious and shooed us out. *Put that away, Eddie!* he'd yelled at him. *Put that away right now!* And I was embarrassed but not in trouble quite as much because I didn't think my mother would really mind if I showed him my innocent pale plump hairless crotch in exchange for a peek at his little pink finger of a thing. It didn't matter back then. But things were different now.

Now they must be longer and rolled up or something in there, to make that bulge like that. But then what were the balls they talked about and joked about? Off to the side? Packed up in there as well? How big?

And where was the hair?

I knew they must have hair down there as I had hair. But my hair was a neat prim triangle. And theirs? I didn't know. Disorganized? All messy?

I'd seen something once; glimpsed the lifeguard dressing in the men's room at the pool. The door flipped open and before the door flipped shut again I saw him—familiar, brown, bronzed grown-up shoulders and his face the same as always but then, below, a dark patch and something that hung down but I couldn't see it clearly and could only rehearse in my mind the flipping open door, dark patch and hanging down thing, door flipping shut—not long enough to see.

And then there was the man who exposed himself to my sister Annie and me on Newark Street. Another clue.

❧

It was a snowy day. We must have been in about fifth or sixth grade, something like that, gone up to People's Drug Store for some notebook paper and peacock blue ink for our Shaefer pens. Coming home we saw a man we didn't recognize walking toward us. We weren't too interested. He was a grown-up. We didn't know him.

His long, beige overcoat just like our father's. Like the overcoats that all men wore.

Flipped open. There again. That's how you found out things. Flipped open. And there was something pink and floppity sticking out and he was holding it and waggling it at us. We went by. I was stunned.

"That was his *penis!*" I said, shocked, to Annie. "Did you see that?"

"It was his thumb," she said.

"His penis!"

"Thumb!"

We looked around again, but he was gone.

✿

Another time, months later. The cookie aisle at the Giant Food Store. I came around a corner and there he was in his coat again.

I knew who it was right away—that man.

My mother had warned me that he did this. *He has a problem.* He was famous for it in our neighborhood, though they only warned him or they couldn't catch him, weren't quite sure of something. I don't know.

He's sick, she'd told me, shaking her head. *He's a sick man. He likes to expose himself to little girls.*

So here he was again, that *sick man,* beside the Oreos, Vienna Fingers.

His coat flipped open. There it was. And there I was—frozen in the cookies. It scared me, but I wasn't sure why. And fascinated me and made me feel strange.

I hurried to the fruit man who stood by the scale beside the oranges.

I tried to tell him.

"In the cookie aisle," I knew the words to say. "A man exposed himself to me."

The man looked angry but I knew he wasn't angry at me, standing there in my winter coat beside the bright oranges.

"Where did he go?" the fruit man asked me in his accent. "I'll get the manager."

But he was gone.

Later my mother invited the police to our house and we sat on the porch and they asked me questions.

They used roundabout language and I didn't know what they were getting at.

"Did he remove the object or did he simply display . . . ?"

I stared at them. I didn't know what they wanted. It was embarrassing.

"Martha, did he take his penis out of his pants?" my mother asked me.

Now that was *really* embarrassing. That was my mother for you.

But at least I knew what she was talking about. And I could say, ashamed and hot-faced, "Yes."

✿

So. This is what I had to work with. Eddie Tinker's tiny finger of a penis under the ping pong table. His father's big,
red, angry face. The bulge in the boys' pants at school. The
dark patch at the swimming pool. The red floppity thing my
sister said was a thumb. The grocery store encounter. The
sexless lump between the boy doll's legs. The pictures in our
PFL book. Not much to go on.

But that didn't stop me from finding some exciting, wonderful connection with the words on the page. Scarlett
O'Hara's heaving bosom. The *soft vee of her crotch* in *Peyton
Place.* The cute boys with their lopsided darling grins and
floppy hair. The bad boy singers slouched together stony-faced
and cruel at the camera. These images all went together. Different words could do it. *Panties. Spanking. Thrusting. Press.*
Even the word *fumbling.* As in *his fingers fumbled with her buttons.* There was something dully pleasurable in that.

That was enough to fuel the dark and secret moments in
my bed alone when I would push my hands between my legs,
roll over, rub and rub, my hot face pressed into the pillow
until the stars paraded by my eyes and I felt done.

Was that it? Was that how it was? But how embarrassing
with someone else! You'd have to get undressed, I thought.
You'd have to show them.

Show them what you had. Which *you* didn't even recog-
nize. Your body. Which you loved but also were ashamed of.
Your breasts were too big. Too small. Too hangy. Too knobby.
One different from the other; lopsided eyes. Look at your

skin. Look at the skin on your thighs! What are those little bumps you get in winter? They look awful—like the skin on a chicken. When you scratch at them they bleed and bleed.

❧

Now, at Madeira, I gauged my own changes by the changes in the bodies all around me. The other girls. Their legs, their thighs, the shape of their different breasts, all as familiar as my own.

Their breasts looked right on them. Inevitable, though they were sometimes unexpected; like Kate having big surprising breasts under her mannish gray wool riding jacket. Or the loping, wolf-faced girl who also had big breasts when you wouldn't think she'd have any at all. The plump, big, wide-assed girl with little flat breasts. The pancake happy breasts of Cassie and the small, pointy firm breasts of Sydney Jane. I was used to them all. They were all around me every day. The teachers with their own breasts and under their clothes their own crotches and behinds, their own plump, winter-colored legs.

The male teachers who must all have penises. They weren't like boys our age who wore tight pants. Their pants were full and loose. Brown corduroy. Beige khaki. So did all their apparatus hang down one leg? How far down? And didn't it twist around and hurt them?

I could have thought about this kind of stuff for hours.

My friends and I didn't discuss it.

We said *he's cute* and let it go at that.

The girls in the locker room, though, they talked about everything. I heard them from behind the clanging lockers.

God, I thought he was going to come right in my face!

He had his hand in my cunt when my father walked in the door!

He wanted me to suck him off in the car!

God. And they all looked so normal.

✿

Was I going to have to do these things? Because that was part of it, I knew. That's what a lot of it was about—the songs and the stuff in the magazines and *The East Village Other* and the R. Crumb comix and the rest of it. A lot of it had to do with sex. I was for Free Love. I must be. It went along with Peace, didn't it? And it had the word *free* in it like civil rights and it was a *right* and the Republicans were against it, so I must be for it, but what exactly did it entail? And how much was I, personally, going to have to contribute?

There was no one to talk to about these things. The other girls all seemed to know what they would or wouldn't do; or else they'd done it all already, like the girls in the locker room. The teachers, all the grown-ups of the world, had their own secrets underneath their clothes. And school wore on and on moving forward with its steady current carrying us all along with it. When would I come to Life?

5

EUGENE McCARTHY & THE RED LEATHER WALLET

BACK WHEN I was at Alice Deal Junior High School, I got a huge crush on a boy with perfect features. One day he came up to me in the hall.

"I heard you were in a protest march," he told me.

Bunches of us from Cleveland Park would go down in station wagons, trudge up and down in front of the White House in the cold dark night. On Saturdays Bishop Moore led us to Lafayette Park where we stood hand in hand with people we didn't know under the cloudy, moody Washington autumn skies.

"Are you against the war in Vietnam?" he asked me.

"Yeah."

We got permission to leave homeroom and go out and argue in the stairwell. Our teachers let us because it was current events. His father was in the government. A general or something.

I got my ammunition from my father.

"There's this boy at school who says we have to fight to keep the Communists from taking over the world."

My father looked up from his evening paper. He was always reading the newspaper—the *New York Times*, the *Washington Post*, the *Post-Dispatch*. At night he'd bring home the *Evening Star* and the *Washington Daily News*. The inky stacks piled up beside his Danish modern chair. His fingers dark with reading.

"Well, it's a bum war, Martha," my father told me.

My father was a foreign correspondent for *The St. Louis Post Dispatch*. He'd been over there tons of times—to Vietnam, to Laos, Cambodia. He said the war in Vietnam was a mistake from the start.

"How come?" I asked him. I was against it because it was a war. But he had real reasons.

"Martha," he told me, "people think there's a Communist conspiracy like an evil octopus trying to take over the world. They think the Russians and the Chinese are working together. That there's a Sino-Soviet conspiracy. They're all wet. Ho Chi Minh has used their help, but he's fighting for freedom and independence.

"And there's another thing—because of what happened in World War II, people think you've got to stop an aggressor in his tracks. But we're not dealing with Hitler here.

"We can't win this war. The North Vietnamese and the Vietcong are fighting for independence and for the unity of their country that's been colonized and split in half by outsiders. They've got a powerful incentive. But most of our soldiers don't want to be there—they're just hoping to get home alive. Our morale is low, but the other side is fighting for survival."

I wasn't sure exactly what he meant by all that Sino-Soviet stuff, but I knew he was right. He'd been there. Everything I knew was about emotion and cute little Vietnamese babies getting shot and children aflame with napalm running down the street, but there was also a logic behind the peace movement—a series of ponderous arguments and explanations that grown-ups used to bolster truth.

I went back the next day and repeated my father's arguments to the boy in the stairwell.

He'd been talking to his father, too. And he had a new set of arguments of his own.

That night I told my father what the boy had said.

"He says I must be a Communist if I'm against the war. He says we have to support our troops."

My father thought for a minute, looking at me seriously.

"Ask him," he said, "if he thinks you should always support any war your country undertakes. Tell him that if he says yes, then there's no reason for further conversation. Because if he thinks we ought to unquestioningly follow our country into war, then there's nothing more to discuss."

I thought about that. It made good sense. But I didn't want to ask the boy that question. Because if he said yes—and he might have—then our morning arguments during homeroom would be over, and I liked the arguing, I liked the feeling of passionate indignation. And I liked his handsome, alien face.

✿

February 1968. The war was still on and Eugene McCarthy was running for president. My parents knew him. He lived in our neighborhood, and he was against the War. He was the first politician since Kennedy that didn't seem like a Republican. Even Johnson sort of seemed like a Republican. And all those other tired, sour old men in the Senate. McCarthy wasn't young like Bobby Kennedy and handsome and rich, but he was handsome in a drifty, gray, Minnesotan way, wise and poetic. And we had to do something to stop the war.

All the rest of them went along with it—the senators and everything—they agreed with it or they didn't really agree, sort of knew it was bad, but they didn't want to look like they were soft on Communism or not patriotic. Everybody was just letting it happen, except my dad, who wrote the truth about it even though the government tapped our phones, and Eugene McCarthy who was running for president and who might actually make things better in the world.

My parents were for him. My dad had a tiny Eugene McCarthy button, which he wore on the underneath side of his lapel because he was a reporter and he couldn't be openly partisan. When my sister and I started volunteering at campaign headquarters, our parents thought it was wonderful that we were *getting involved politically*. I felt proud and important. And besides, a lot of cute guys worked there.

On Saturdays Annie and I helped out at the McCarthy for President office at Alban Towers, the tall brown brick apartment building on Wisconsin Avenue. We collated papers and stuffed envelopes with the other volunteers. The radio was on WEAM; and most of them were in college.

There were some kids there, too. Paul Wright, the handsome one I'd danced with at the Mayflower Hotel, was working there, and a guy named Steve with curly hair who'd dropped out of high school in Massachusetts to work for McCarthy. My sister Annie and our friend Kathleen.

In February a bunch of us took a bus to New Hampshire to help with the primary there. We slept on a church floor and went door-to-door for McCarthy through the Manchester snow, and over spring vacation I went out to Wisconsin. Paul Wright was there, and other volunteers all working out of old hotel rooms, walking down the snowy streets of Milwaukee in the wintertime—*We'd like to talk to you about Senator McCarthy, he's running for president.* Wouldn't it be cool if he won?

I was part of something big, something new that brought people together. It wasn't just like war protesting which was fun, but sort of disorganized and angry and at the end of it—what had you done? The people behind the barricades still mad at us—*Go live in Russia!* This was different. This was a grown-up endeavor. Everybody there was funny and cool. Smart college guys with beards or with no beards. With their sleeves rolled back who went to Yale and Harvard. With corduroy pants and self-assurance. Who drank coffee, smoked cigarettes. Looked like men but acted sometimes like boys and thought I was terrific.

How old are you, anyway? they'd ask me. They thought it was cute that I was only sixteen.

✦

We went out all day canvassing the icy roads of Milwaukee; walking from house to house slumped under in the snow.

The people were friendlier here than in New Hampshire.

"Oh, you must be cold, come in!" the lady in the doorway said to us.

And, "all the way from Washington?" and shook her head. "Well, you must really believe in what you're doing."

We did! We did! Vindicated by the lady on the green sofa. We did! We believed in it. We were against the war and we were doing something. We were going to get rid of Johnson. *Hey! Hey! LBJ! How many kids did you kill today?* We were against the corrupt political System. We were for civil rights. We were for freedom. We were for Eugene McCarthy who was so quiet and unusual, not a typical politician but a poet, and he'd stop the war.

I felt proud and determined. "This is really important. Your vote can make a difference in the world," I said, looking her right in the eye.

The man I was with looked startled, glanced around at me. They never let young ones like me go out alone. We had to go with someone older. Someone who was at least in college.

"That was a good thing you did in there," he told me later as we went out into the puddles and frozen fields of Milwaukee.

We turned and she waved to us from the doorway.

"You maybe even got us a vote."

"You think she'll vote for McCarthy?"

He shrugged. "You never know. But she wouldn't have before. Now we've got a shot at it."

He stopped. There was a broad field before us. Patchy with snow and the flat winter grass underneath sticking through in beigey patches here and there. It was late March.

"You ever fly a kite?" he asked me.

"Huh?"

"A kite. This would be a perfect place to fly a kite. I used to fly kites with my father when I was a kid."

And I understood that he was telling me something else, was accepting me into his own uncertain ranks. Adult. When you looked back at stuff like that. Stuff you used to do.

But I didn't know. Wasn't I still a kid? What happened? Was it over already?

❧

I hadn't eaten hardly anything in about five days. I was going to be really thin. I hurried out to canvass with people they assigned to me; typed letters for the staff at the Sheraton Shroeder. Ran back to the Milwaukee Hotel to man the desk with Steve and Paul.

Paul had gotten his hair cut.

"Clean for Gene," he said.

"God," said Steve. "God, man, you look like somebody else."

He did look different, but he was still handsome.

I smoked the same cigarettes as Paul now. Lucky Strikes. Filterless. Steve smoked them, too. I put my pack down in the hotel coffee shop on the shiny Formica counter that looked spangled in the coffee shop light with the cake holders and the napkin holders and the plastic-covered Midwestern menus with the metal tips. I felt expansive sitting there, adult, with my pack of cigarettes, no sleep, my gritty eyes.

"Just coffee," I told the lady. "Black."

"You don't want anything to eat?"

No. I didn't want anything. I wanted to be so thin I disappeared. I wanted to be the opposite of myself. I wanted to be thin and racked with a racking cough. I wanted to be huddled in my coat against the northern wintry blasts, a lonely grown-up. I had a whole picture of who I was, here in Milwaukee.

✿

We stayed up late that night in the tall lobby of the Milwaukee Hotel with the dark paneling and the plump dark red velvet chairs. It was exotic, being in a downtown hotel at night, halfway across the country from home, with the abandoned snowy streets and neon bars outside.

We sprawled out in the chairs, Paul, Steve, and I, talking about everything, even girls. Paul told about this girl he'd been in love with. She was older and she'd hurt him.

"I guess I'm not really over her yet," he said.

That was so sad! Maybe that's why he had that faraway look when I met him at the dance.

"I know what you mean," I told him. I tried to think of

somebody I'd been in love with. Maybe I could use Jon. But he didn't really count. Everybody else already had some sad, past history. I better hurry.

Outside the quiet snow fell down. The lobby was deserted. We might have been anywhere, in any time. The downtown, old-fashioned city. The USO headquarters next door. The coffee shop with its Formica counters, silent now. The Midwest winter drifting into spring.

"Let's go back to the hotel," Paul said at last.

We walked back through the snowy, cold night streets, talking and laughing, leaping the murky puddles. We were all tired and bumping into each other as we walked, clutching each other to keep from falling down. And then, suddenly, we were at the Sheraton Shroeder, tall and bright in the city night.

Paul glanced at Steve.

"I've got to meet someone," Steve said, and he disappeared.

◈

We were up in the room where Paul was staying with a bunch of guys. Nobody else was there.

"You want to watch TV?" Paul asked me.

"OK," I said.

I didn't know what was supposed to happen next. It felt as if it were up to me.

He turned on the TV.

There were beds all over the room, but nobody else was there.

He would kiss me or not kiss me.

I could wait, but then it might never happen. I might have to be the one.

But what did I do? How did I start it—that slow swim?

There were no parents here. There was no one to call down from upstairs. No one to hear us. There was only the dark huge hotel room full of unmade beds and the big television showing some old black-and-white movie and the abandoned room service trays and the boy beside me sitting on the bed and it was late.

I could feel the hum of his body near mine. Could feel how his hair would feel; the tender edges. How it would feel for his hands to touch me.

Everything rushed around us and was done.

Everything seemed inevitable and certain.

And all I really wanted was to be there with him now, with everything about to happen.

☙

He had the front of my dress pulled down and his mouth on my breast when the door opened and we could see the tall dark shapes of the boys in the doorway.

Paul pulled my dress up; yanked the blanket over us both.

I started giggling and he put his hand over my mouth.

"You okay?" somebody shouted.

"Sure," Paul told him in a tired voice that said it all. Boy language. *I had her clothes partly off. You interrupted us. I could have, maybe would have, but then you barged in.*

But to me in the dark he was elegant. Courteous.

"Are you okay?" he whispered.

I tightened my arm around him the way I imagined a woman would tighten her arm around a man.

And we fell asleep like that with all our clothes on and Paul's arm around me and my face against his chest, which felt like a man's chest. That was really what I wanted anyway, that and the brief sight of my own breast in the dim room. That and his head bent over me tenderly. That and the expectation and the TV flickering away with the sound off and the quiet distant thump of the night snow falling from the roof of the hotel.

❦

The next night Paul lay on top of me with all our clothes on and ground himself against me again and again. There was a name for this. I didn't know it. Ground himself against me until it kind of hurt, but it also felt good in a dark, fierce way.

I couldn't believe it. Here I was—Martha Dudman—grinding away with Paul Wright, the most handsome boy I had ever seen in my life with his perfect features, his rich, important father, his big Catholic family. His big happy important family and he had chosen me! *I* was the one he was grinding away at in the dark hotel room. *I* was the one he did the Temptation Walk with in the lobby of the Milwaukee Hotel. *I* was the one whose hand he took almost as if by accident and squeezed when Steve said something funny. *I* was the one he looked around at, smiled at. It was like a dream.

It was like a dream of a dream. Better than anything I

could have made up in a story. Could have made up late at night trying to get to sleep imagining this perfect world full of handsome boys and near sex and the dim romantic veiled desire of Milwaukee.

✿

Then it was over. Back to reality and back to school. Back on the bus and the girls' faces and the dull, slow start of spring and classes with the same weary linoleum floor and all the world just beyond the windows and the whole dull time of it; the boring stupidity of it; the plod of it! None of them knew anything about it—anything I'd seen! Anything I knew! McCarthy, any of it, Vietnam. Didn't know about the grown men I'd talked to late in the night—talked about the things grown-ups talked about; politics, deep stuff, philosophy, ideas. But here was the same dull treadmill, the same small frilly phony debutante whirl of horses, boyfriends, diets, and geometry, of drinking on the weekends, parties, boys. They didn't know a thing.

My life was outside of here. My real life. I wanted the fullness of it. I wanted the red leather wallet.

✿

Years before, when I was seven or eight, I had started stealing things. I hadn't done it very often, but I could still remember the sensation. The craving. The hungry, secret feeling; wanting things of the adult world: car keys, jackknives. One time, at the Cleveland Park Club ladies' dressing room, a red leather wallet.

Nobody locked anything up in 1959. You could go to the pool house and take your clothes off and leave them neatly folded on the shelf with your wallet right on top—a thick red leather billfold full of the mysteries of adult womanhood. Driver's license. Ticket stubs. Photographs of your friends. Money. But it was not the money I was after.

❧

I am alone in the pale green dressing room. Afternoon light comes in through the window and the cement floor is cool and rough.

I see her clothes on the shelf, the clothes of the other women, the wallet. I want it. She used to be my baby-sitter. I want to be her: grown-up and with a wallet.

I'm barefoot. We have to leave our shoes outside the chain-link fence.

I stare at the red leather wallet; that thick wad of the grown-up world. Then I take it. I put it down the front of my shorts, but it sticks out too much, so I roll it up in my towel with my damp bathing suit, and I go out.

Past the dim room where the shower is, along the narrow corridor with puddles on the floor and outside, past the men's room. And is this the time the door flips open and I see the lifeguard with no clothes on? Or is this a different time? Which time is it? Patchy dark hair? Stolen wallet? My father waiting. *You took such a long time in there, Martha.*

I can see her swimming in the pool back and forth with

the long, slow laps that ladies take in the late afternoon when all the splashing and the Marco Polo is done. The grown-up hour when the grown-ups swim.

✿

My mother turns from the phone, her face is silent.

Martha, I need to talk to you.

But by now I have forgotten all about it.

I don't connect her phone call with the secret, dark, deep, buried place inside me where the wallet lies.

I came home and hid the wallet way back in my closet.

As I put it away, I'd felt the thrill again. The quivering silence in the dressing room just before I took it. The silence of the house around me. The silence of my room. My secret silence. As if everything, even the backyard where the damp towels hung on the line, even the street where the cars went by, even the trees and the sounds of my mother in the kitchen—everything, at last everything, were stilled by my action. As if there were some power. The power of the red wallet. The power of my having taken it.

But I have forgotten all that now.

Now it is late in the day and I am thinking about something else. Dinner. Hot dogs. Story time.

Did you take Suzie Taylor's wallet out of the ladies' dressing room this afternoon at the Cleveland Park Club?

I draw in; grow very quiet.

Then, *yes.*

Oh, Martha!

There is silence in the kitchen, but it is a different silence now. Not the good, strong, powerful silence I made. This is the cold, still silence of punishment. The light comes in through the big windows. Big and bright. The kitchen feels cold with the light, even now in summer.

Where is it?

In my room.

I'm not going to tell her where. I might need to save that secret place for other things.

Go get it, Martha.

And then, later, there are all the things that you find out come after. After the secret longing. After the guilty pleasure. After that one bright moment when you're taking it and the ladies' dressing room is so still with a magic stillness that you have created and you hold that thick red wallet in your hand.

I stole it.

Stole it! my mother howls at me, belt in her hand, coming in later to whip me. Her face looks torn.

I cower against the bureau. I am terrified.

She's crying. She's yelling at me. Yelling *Stolen!* Yelling *You stole!* and crying and I'm crying too and she's flailing out at me with the belt and I'm scared. She's so angry and so sad. It doesn't even hurt.

Later that night I write other things in my diary. *I love Randy Evans,* I write. *I can't wait for school so I can see him.*

But I know. I know what I am.

6

SHOOTING THE BUFFALO

McCARTHY GOT 57 percent of the vote in Wisconsin. Johnson started negotiations with North Vietnam. We'd done something. We were changing history! Sacrificing our hair, our dirty jeans, our patchy jackets, our bellbottoms— sacrificing our weekends and our youth. We were inside the machine—inside it!—we were working from within.

But there was still so much to do. So much was wrong. The government, big business, everything. It was all linked together. There were people who actually *wanted* the war. Who were profiting from it. Who only pretended that it was about freedom and rights and stuff. And there were people who knew it was wrong but didn't speak up because it wasn't good politics. I asked my father how he could stand it—all the corruption, all the hypocrisy, all the bad guys in the government.

"But there are good guys, too," he told me. "We're just chipping away."

And there I was too, chipping away beside him. And we got 57 percent of the vote and we were winning, but now Bobby Kennedy had to come sneaking in, riding on his brother's bloodstained coattails. We had our man: Eugene McCarthy. We had our own tall, stooped, grey-haired god with his diffident, quizzical Minnesotan face. We had our man with his serious son and his shiny daughters and his sad, mysterious wife. We had our man and we had gone to New Hampshire for him, our unlikely prince. We had gone to Milwaukee for him. We had ground in the hotel rooms for him, licked stamps for him, we walked the snowy streets and we would go on and further for McCarthy and maybe we would win and all be politicians—young warriors of equality and peace.

Then Martin Luther King got shot. He was thirty-seven years old.

Everything was swept away under the great swell of rage from the other side of the city—the Black swell and the white liberal . . . embarrassment. Our horror. Our *distress,* which seemed like such a frilly, prissy thing—useless, phantom, vain.

We watched the news. They were rioting. It was *They* now.

We had no part in this. We were in the system. We were white. We were okay for the civil rights marches; for the Selma, for the White House *Jim Crow must go* round and round in the Washington night with our signs. But we would never be Black and this was *their* sorrow, and he was *their* man.

Paul and Steve returned from Milwaukee.

We watched the news. They were rioting. The streets of Washington boiled and heaved.

There was a curfew at five o'clock.

There were soldiers all over the place.

We huddled in my parents' house and Paul and Steve had to spend the night because no one was allowed to go even the few blocks to Paul's house. We were prisoners. *Yippee.*

We were at war.

"They're coming over the bridge!" came one report and it was so weird because who were *they* and who were *we* and didn't they know—I thought they knew—we were their friends?

And then it was all confusing and scary but also wonderfully exciting and dramatic. Paul and Steve were at my house and they couldn't leave and my mother could do nothing about it and my father could do nothing but bring down the sleeping bags from the attic and we were all there with the television on and we watched the news: looters and fires and people pushing and crazy right in our city like it was some foreign city; like some weird place where we had never lived.

Where were the Black ladies who came by bus to clean the houses of our neighborhood?

Where were the regular Black people, the ones we knew from Sunday school, from junior high, the ones that they imported to Madeira? Where were they in all of that dark, angry swirl?

We lay on the rug and we watched television and we were part of history. *This is part of history.* we told each other.

Teargas.

Soldiers.

Troops in the streets.

The National Guard.

We lay on the living room floor watching bits and pieces of the action on my parents' six-inch Sony TV screen.

"Is that all you have?" Paul asked. He came from a big family with lots of kids and an enormous color television set.

"We don't watch television much," I mumbled, embarrassed by our shabby life.

He was right next to me but he didn't touch me. Maybe because Steve was there.

Looters. Rioting. *I have a dream. Roll over on top of me, please Paul.* I wanted to feel his weight. But he was distant. He was different now, here, back in Washington, though he and Steve slept on the living room floor and ate waffles at my mother's breakfast table.

"We better go back to my house," he told me later and he didn't look at me. Something was wrong. *I'll call you later,* I wanted him to say, but he didn't say it.

They went off. Steve tall and funny looking with his curly hair and his long, blue-jeaned legs. Paul competent and handsome and smiling and silent.

They didn't call.

I had to go to school but they didn't call.

The next weekend they didn't come by the Sandal Shop where I was working.

They didn't call.

I went to headquarters on Sunday but they weren't there.

The war was over. The streets of Washington were blank and quiet.

Burned out storefronts and police bands tied across. Old sawhorses and quiet, empty sidewalks. It looked and it didn't look like the city I'd grown up in. It looked as if it had been abandoned, broken, and that it would never be the same again. I felt like a foreigner in my own town.

✿

On Palm Sunday a bunch of people from our neighborhood went to a special service at a Black church on the other side of Sixteenth Street where Bishop Moore preached. We walked through the streets of Washington carrying palms through the ruined neighborhoods. The charred store doorways like black eyes; the broken windows and the tattered curtains blowing out into the air. Soldiers stood at attention on the sidewalk with their guns. Black ones and white ones both together staring straight ahead. They were young. They weren't even men. They were just boys trying to look solemn.

We trooped along. All the Black somber people of the church and we few white ones trooping along with our palm fronds, and I wasn't sure what it was all about. I didn't really get this Christian stuff, their stories. But it was nice, I thought. Like we were doing something. With our palms. Showing support or something; white and Black. But did they even want us there at all?

✿

Finally I called him.
"Is Paul there?"

His mother on the phone.

"He's gone to the movies," she said to me. His guard dog.
I felt like saying, "Oh I'm sorry."

I didn't leave my name. I was ashamed. Girls weren't supposed to call boys up.

I don't think it's a good idea, my mother had told me.

What did she know? But I knew it myself. I knew it from
the shrinking feeling as if I'd stolen something. Like I had
done something embarrassing and hot-faced, weird. Calling
him up. Not leaving my name. Him knowing. His mother
knowing. All his sisters knowing and knowing with their
jaunty names—Kat, Rita—whatever their names were—
jaunty, short Catholic girls' names with their happy, big-
family wide-screen TV faces. I could just see them lying
around in the living room, calling over the back of the couch.

Who was that, Ma?

Some girl for Paul.

*Oooooooh—I bet it was Martha Dudman. Was it that girl
Martha, Ma?*

Yes, I think so, grimly.

Wait'll I tell Paul!

And then all of them telling and laughing about me and
teasing him and him getting that handsome, distant, pensive
look, and then what? Defending me? Saying *she's really nice,*
but more likely him laughing too and saying *I know I know*
and shaking his head and all of them making it worse, teasing him, *can't you get rid of her?* And him not being able to get
rid of me, but then why did he grind away at me like that?
Why did he kiss me? Why did his arm go around me and he

pull the covers up over my breasts in that dark hotel room when the boys arrived in the doorway? Didn't that mean anything? Wasn't that love?

✿

I called him again, a few days later.

"I wondered if you wanted to come over."

My mother wasn't there. My father wasn't there. My sister, gone.

"Yeah, sure, I guess so."

"Is Steve still there?"

"He's going back tomorrow. I'll be there in a little bit."

✿

I met him at the door. He was so handsome but was also, after all my longing, all my expectation somehow . . . diminished. Smaller than I'd thought him. Paler.

"Want to go to the garage?" I asked him. "We've got this kind of clubhouse there."

I had imagined how it would be in the garage. We'd sit there and smoke cigarettes with the dim light coming through the trees at the little window. It would be so quiet. We'd be awkward at first, but then we'd be the way we were before.

We'd talk about Milwaukee.

Do you remember, Martha? he'd ask me. And I would, I would!

♦

Only it wasn't like that.

We walked back across the wet spring yard where my sister and I used to play softball; where Jenny Truesdale and I used to act out complicated games; the settlers trekking across America around and around in the damp backyard. The balky mules, the young girl who got a terrible fever and had to be carried in the wagon, the attack of the sexy Indians, making the fire, shooting the buffalo, the thin gray gruel on the wintry morn.

We lit our cigarettes. I sat down on the couch, but he stayed standing, slouched against the wall.

"I can't stay long," he told me.

I looked at him in the dim light.

"I'm going to a party. I'm bringing the—uh—refreshments," he said.

I knew he meant pot, though I'd never smoked it with him, and just a few times, actually, myself.

I wanted to have the kind of talk with him where I told him how I felt and he told me how he felt—which would be the way I wanted him to feel.

I wanted to say the one right thing that would make him realize how much he loved me, but I couldn't think of anything. I just sat on the couch and I smoked and he slouched by the wall and he smoked and he told me Steve was leaving the next day and I said, "Oh can I go to the airport with you?" and he said, "yes," but I could tell he didn't really want me to go, but he was too polite.

After he smoked his cigarette he said, "I really do have to go," and he came over and kissed the top of my head and then he left and I stayed there on the lumpy couch in the chilly garage and smoked my cigarette and then went back across the damp grass to the house.

My mother was in the kitchen. She asked me to set the table. It was time to eat.

✿

My mother. Lately she'd been getting on my nerves. She was always there at every turn with her rules and her questions and her glances. She didn't understand that I was grown-up now. She made me mad.

I used to think she was invincible, triumphant. She looked like Jackie Kennedy, I thought when I was little, with her black hair and her dark eyes and her red lipstick mouth, driving our Studebaker Lark with the top down and her sunglasses on sunny days. Sometimes she got mad at us—our messy rooms, my lousy grades, or when we borrowed her sewing scissors and didn't put them back—but I always had the sense that she would do anything, anything at all, to keep me safe.

If there's a war, my mother told us, *I'll come find you.*

There were triangular black and yellow signs on every building. It meant there was an air raid shelter there.

We had air raid drills at John Eaton Elementary School. The air raid alarm was different from the bright, sharp, normal sound of the fire drill bell—was high-pitched, mean.

The younger children were taken to the school cellar, deep below the normal basement, to a darker, danker place. Sat in their rows of chairs. *Now don't be frightened.*

The older children, fourth and up, were led to the "lower level" outside the art room and the audio-visual room where we watched rickety reels about volcanoes in Hawaii and the honest workers in South America cutting the sugar cane bent over in the hot sun, while the man's newsreel voice read out the facts to us—those exports, imports, population things that made no sense. Then, to personalize it, "Little Juan lives with his family in a mud house on the banks of the Amazon River!"

No mud house would survive what we had coming. The bomb. The joke word. Scary word. The A-Bomb. Nuclear Weapon. When it came it would destroy the world.

And so we were led down while all around the screaming, high-pitched whine continued; led down to kneel with our arms over our heads. Carole Henderson said she nearly fainted. It made her sick, she said, to stay like that.

I didn't mind it, really. It was dark and private there beneath my arms. The quiet children kneeling all around me. A sort of religious feeling, like a special rite. My own deep smell. We stayed low for so long our faces on our knees dreaming our odd, silent, separate dreams. The teacher's voice somewhere above, beyond us, saying things. Reminding us *no, not yet, stay down.*

I wouldn't stay there. I'd come find you, my mother told us.

She was working for the National Symphony Orchestra. She wouldn't stay there, in the tiny dark office across from the hairdresser's with its smell of hairspray, Liz Taylor movie magazines, and Eddie Fisher.

I'd come and find you.

And so I pictured her, my mother, six feet tall, but taller in the image that I had of her—enormous—striding through the ruins of bombed-out Washington, coming to find us. Her legs as tall as tree trunks. The buildings all disheveled and abandoned, blown apart and fallen over; people huddled, scrinched up in the cellars but my mother—savior, tyrant, tall as Atlas—coming through the rubble to find her girls.

And how it would cower before her! Like the waitress at Avignon Frère when my mother slapped her hand on the table and said in her warrior tone, *What's taking so long? We've been sitting here for forty-five minutes!* Like the nurses who wanted to do another test on me when we'd both had it, *Forget it!* she shouted fiercely, *I'm taking this girl home!* Like me, like my sister, cowering in our rooms while our mother in the hallway loomed furious and vengeful, *What am I going to do with you girls? What kind of pigsty do we live in? I don't ask much. I don't ask you girls to go out and get a job. Some parents do that. I only ask you to do well in school and to pick up your rooms! That's all I ask!*

The rumble of furious thunder. The roar of the tornado approaching. The trouble, trouble. But now my mother would not be furious with us. Would be coming to save us. To reach through the abandoned landscape of the ruined city. Would be coming to get us, grab us up forever, once again forever in her big strong arms.

7

CRYING AT
PALISADES PARK

I ALWAYS KNEW my parents loved me and would protect me, but now there was starting to be a sourness between us. They didn't like the way I dressed. They didn't like my friends. They didn't understand the way I was now. The only thing they liked was that I was working for McCarthy. That I was doing something worthwhile, not just hanging around. They were all for us working in the campaign, travelling around to the primaries. Canvassing suburban neighborhoods. Handing out leaflets. Typing press releases. Building crowds. They thought it was wonderful that we were politically active. So when Annie and I wanted to go work in the New York primary when school got out, they were delighted. They didn't know a thing.

The McCarthy for President office on Columbus Circle was a mess of desks and people and young guys with curly hair.

"Your name?" a lady asked. "Do you have housing?"

I didn't have housing. I didn't want to stay with a family friend like my sister Annie; eat breakfast with them, be in at a certain time for them, call my parents with them smiling at me from the couch or something. *God.*

"She can stay with us," a man said.

He had sideburns. He wasn't very tall, but he was handsome in a sort of cocky New York way.

"We can put somebody up," he told us.

He was nineteen, he said. Jeff Weiss. Went to NYU. Lived out in Westchester.

"I can get you out there. I've got a car," he told me, carelessly.

"Don't worry," he said, "I'll call my mom. I'm living with my parents and my brother's away this summer. You can have his room."

Okay, I thought. He was handsome. He was nice. He was nineteen. He had a car. And his mom would be there.

Somebody came through and rumpled my hair. "Well look who's here! You gonna help us beat Kennedy?"

I was home.

We drove away in Jeff's old MG convertible—dark red and so small it felt as if we could drive right under the bellies of the trucks.

"God, do you ever do that?" I asked him.

He laughed. He acted like everything I said was funny.

"How old are you anyway?" he asked me.

"Sixteen."

He told me he'd just been kidding around when he said he was nineteen. He was really only seventeen himself; got into NYU early. "But I didn't want to say I was seventeen. I thought you were some hip nineteen-year-old chick."

I felt as if I might be nineteen; now that I was in New York.

I was glad I'd worn my dress with the big sleeves and the orange flowers on it. Glad I wasn't fat. Glad my hair turned out that morning.

"How long have you worked for McCarthy?"

Jeff lived way out in Westchester in a row of houses that all looked exactly the same. His father was a psychiatrist. His mother was nice. Everybody was nice. They seemed to expect me to be there.

We ate supper but it wasn't like my house with every-thing—every look, every potato—taking on an enormous weight of its own. It was just supper with people that I didn't know. Then the parents went to bed and Jeff and I stayed up to watch the California primary on TV. There were two La-Z-Boy recliners facing the television set in the den and we sat side by side staring at the screen.

By the time Bobby Kennedy was assassinated we were making out.

❦

Jeff and I made out in the rec room in his basement. We made out on the damp grass of the schoolyard a few blocks away. We made out in his little car, leaning across from our bucket seats with the emergency brake stabbing me in the side. I thought about him at the McCarthy office all day long.

I felt like a grown-up. I never wanted to go to sleep. I started taking No Doz, which was sort of like drinking lots of coffee, only quicker. I found some pills in Jeff's dad's medicine cabinet. There were a whole bunch of them, so I took a lot, and put them in a little film case. I think they were some kind of speed. They were long and yellow and they made me feel wonderful and clear and sharp and funny, and I didn't have to hardly sleep at all.

I rode into town with Jeff or Jeff's father, worked at the office, and ran around New York City with some of the guys from the campaign. My sister was around, but I hardly ever saw her. This was exactly how I wanted to be: sharp and funny and daring and smoking cigarettes in New York City, making out in a parked car in the suburbs like a regular teenage girl, not always thinking thinking thinking.

❦

But sometimes the pills made me feel too weird. One night Jeff took me with some friends to Palisades Park and I started crying in the parking lot and couldn't stop.

"I can't go in there," I kept sobbing, staring at the bright lights and the roller coaster and the crowds of people—all those cars and the cliffs on the other side of the river that were *too high,* I kept saying, *too high.*

"Oh she's just wrecked," Jeff said disgustedly to his friend, Tommy.

Tommy looked bored. He was Japanese.

Tommy's girlfriend, who had been nice to me before, when we were eating pizza at Tommy's house and doing the dishes, looked embarrassed.

"Come on, Martha," she kept saying. "It's okay. Come on."

"You go!" I shouted, crying unreasonably. We'd all come in one car. What could they do, just leave me there in the parking lot with all the other cars that glinted in the night?

"Come on," Jeff said at last, and took me roughly by the shoulder and shoved me back into the car. "Let's take her home."

Then he could go back out. Back out with normal friends. It had been my mistake, trying to act like I was normal too. I was all mixed up with the long yellow pills that I'd been taking and the hash I'd smoked at Tommy's and the Boone's Farm wine.

"Come on," Tommy's girlfriend kept telling me. "Come on, try it, it's good."

She was so nice and now I'd ruined everything.

"Let's get her home," Jeff said and wouldn't look at me the whole way back in the car.

I left the next morning without seeing him.

There was a big mailing that had to go out, and I wound up working late at McCarthy headquarters and not getting back out to Westchester. I slept a few hours on a couch in the back room, and then worked the whole next day, propped up on No Doz and the yellow pills. My sister looked at me in the office with a quizzical expression.

"What's going on?" she asked me, but I didn't tell. I felt kind of weird, but I knew I'd be okay if I could sleep. I was just so tired.

🌀

I was deep asleep that night when Jeff came into his brother's room where I was staying. I woke up disoriented and there he was. He was only wearing his underpants. I could see him standing by the bed in the faint, odd light from the street-light. The bluish, chemical light made his skin glow strangely. Made him look as if he were on a black-and-white television screen late at night.

His parents were just down the hall. His brother's match-box cars were lined up on a shelf beside the twin bed where I slept. The only boy I'd seen in underpants before was Eddie Tinker under the ping pong table. It had always been dark.

"Hi," he said quietly.

How long had he been standing there, staring down at me?

I was confused. I'd gotten stoned with one of the guys that afternoon in Central Park, and then the pills wore off. Suddenly I was exhausted. As if someone had dropped me from a great, tall distance. Thud.

I'd come in late by taxi. Jeff had already been in bed when I arrived.

And now he was here, standing above me in the dim light of his brother's room. I was so tired. I just wanted to slide back down into sleep.

He got into the bed with me. The skin of his shoulder felt cool and damp, like the skin of a corpse beside me. It was a hot night. I was wearing only my underpants and a T-shirt. He started touching me right away. Not kissing me, just touching me. His touch felt angry and imperious, like it was his turn now. Like my turn had been the sweet beginning kisses on the couch. Holding hands. Stroking my hair. Girl things. Putting his arm around me. Now he got to do what he wanted to do—squeeze my breasts like they were something that he wanted to grab and tear at. Put his hand between my legs and rub me through my underpants and then right away without even waiting or saying anything, sticking his hand inside my underpants, shoving his fingers inside me. He was just like Jon.

It felt scary. It felt good. I didn't know what it felt. I was so sleepy and confused by the odd light in the room, by this new person.

"Come on," he told me. "Come on."

He grabbed my hand and put it on the thick ridge in his underpants and made me rub it. He rubbed my hand back and forth over it and it was hard and large and rigid and I wasn't sure what I was supposed to be doing, but I didn't have to know anything, because he moved my hand for me up and down.

"Come on," he kept saying, "come on," but he didn't say my name. Not once.

He pulled his own underpants down and then I was

touching the smooth bare flesh of his penis. So smooth it was like a dream. I would have liked to have touched it slowly, thought about the texture of it, looked it over, if it hadn't been so embarrassing to even think of looking at a boy's penis when he was right there. Maybe if he could just go out of the room and leave me here with it, then I could get a look at this mysterious thing. Finally. I could find out all about it. How it worked. The skin of it! Unbelievable! It was so smooth, so almost silky. And under that smooth skin the rubbery hardness of him. That, too, and the little cap at the end. This was so different from what I'd glimpsed in my limited repertoire of actual penis history.

Different from the flapping thumb of a thing that the man in the Giant Food Store wagged at me in the cookie aisle.

Different from the pointy, narrow ruler of a thing that Jon Bragdon tried to stick into me in the darkness of my parents' living room.

Different from Paul Wright's unseen lump grinding into me at the Sheraton Shroeder.

No, this was it. A man's whole penis right here— revealed, finally, in the pearly dark.

I wanted to lay my face against it. I wanted to run my fingers lightly over it. I wanted to lick it, touch it, sniff it, know it, investigate it—but he wouldn't let me. He rubbed my hand up and down, back and forth fiercely, stubbornly, as if together we were on some furious assignment to rub and rub it clean.

"Come on!" he said again in his gruff, angry voice. "Come on! Come on!" And then, suddenly, he reached over, pulled my underpants down and rolled over on top of me, all clammy and heavy and slick and firm against me.

"No!" I whispered. I was all confused, snatched out of my dreamy reverie.

"No!" again as he tried to push my legs apart with his strong legs.

Suddenly he tensed against me. His whole body straightened and he stretched out hard on top of me. He seemed to almost get lighter, as if the spasm running through his body had lifted him right off of me—it was that strong.

I didn't make a sound. He shuddered, and collapsed upon me. Heavy, leaden, weighty, and impossible.

I didn't move.

He lay there for a moment, and then rolled off and lay beside me, breathing hard.

We didn't say a thing.

The room was quiet.

"Jeff?" I whispered finally, reaching out toward him.

"God!" he whispered back. "You don't know anything, do you?" Got up and went out of the room.

I lay there. My underpants were pulled down partway and my belly was wet with some thick goo that soon began to dry there to a crackly paste, like the paste we used to get at school. When it dried it got all cracked and weird and crunchy at the edges. Howie Reifsnyder used to make little patties out of it in the fourth grade. He'd dry them on his desk and eat them, my sister told me once. I hardly knew him. He was in her class.

✿

The next morning Jeff was gone when I got up. It was late morning. The middle of the day.

Maybe it was a Saturday, I don't remember. When I came downstairs Jeff's mother was in the kitchen like any mother would be, anywhere.

"Oh, hi, dear," she said like she didn't know anything. Maybe she didn't. Know about the long yellow pills I'd been stealing out of the medicine cabinet. Know about me crying at Palisades Park. Know about Jeff coming into my room at night and what we'd done there. Know about what I had washed off in the shower; that weird paste.

"How about some toast?" she asked me.

She was nice. They were all nice. I couldn't wait to get away. I felt as if I'd stolen something. Stolen their son.

8

THE ROCKY GODDAM
SHORE

ANNIE WAS AT McCarthy headquarters. It was two days until the New York primary. We weren't going to win.

"Let's go to Maine," Annie said. "Let's surprise The Parents. We can fly student stand-by to Bangor for twenty-five dollars."

I looked around at the office. It was so messy and familiar. I liked it here, but how could I keep staying at Jeff's?

"Yeah," I said. "Okay. Let's go."

So we flew up out of New York City's hot and dusty murk up northward across New England to Maine where life was simple.

Maine was always the same. Blue sparkly sky. Blue spangly sea. Slap and snap of the sail. Crash of waves on the rocky shore. Simple. Safe. Snug. Fireside and big hard sleep after a whole day picking blueberries and riding bicycles and rowing boats; exploring the island and getting your feet all wet in a bog somewhere deep in the woods. Pine trees. Pine pillows. Pie.

✿

I was glad to get away from Jeff. He'd barely talked to me since that terrible night in his brother's bedroom. I'd been away a lot; staying in the city.

"Working," I told his mother. She hugged me at the door.

"Take care, Martha," she said. "Help our man win."

She didn't say anything about any of the rest of it—the stolen pills, the stains on the sheet. Didn't she know?

"I'll try," I said, like everything was normal.

Nothing was normal. Everything was inside out and upside down.

I wanted to go to Maine with my sister and my family and have everything the way it was supposed to be. The way it used to be when I was young.

✿

But then of course it wasn't. The island, which had always seemed enormous and wonderful and full of possibilities, seemed small and shabby.

I didn't feel oblivious anymore—the way you are when

you're a kid, when you just play with your stuff and don't pay any attention to the grown-up world.

Now the teenagers on the dock all stared at me. Everybody knew everybody else, but I didn't know any of them.

They're all Republicans, I said to myself. They're all straight. They're all rich preppies. They were all in their summer polo shirts and Bermuda shorts. The odd, old fadey plaids that preppies wore. Their flops of blond, flat, preppie hair. Later they would all go out in their preppie sailboats: Bulls Eyes, Mercuries, or go water-skiing in their preppie bathing suits behind their Boston Whalers. They were all a certain way. But at least they knew how they were.

I didn't know what I was like—if I was a Madeira girl, if I was a hippie. If I was a snappy political person in the McCarthy campaign who sent speeches by telex and could talk to grown-ups. I didn't know if I was sophisticated or shy; if I was daring and sexy or lumpy and dull.

I didn't know how to be in Maine the way I was now.

The island always used to make me feel safe and like a kid, but in a good way. My sister and I wore whatever we wore; old jeans and cutoffs, T-shirts. Now suddenly it mattered what I wore and how I acted. It was just like being back in Washington.

My mother looked at me with her sad, reproachful eyes.

"You really hurt my feelings, Martha, the way you treat me."

This was not the way she used to speak to me when I was little. She used to just know everything. Now she looked softer. Older. I didn't want to think about how she looked or how she felt. I wanted to get away from her reproach and anger and her supplication. It covered me up. It made it hard to breathe. I was suffocating here with her and her serious face.

And even my dad. My dad who had always been my favorite. Who gave me the yardstick to judge all other men. Could they fix things—fix anything—the way my dad could? Were they always nice? Did they never get mad? Did they know everything? Could they tell stories? Did they have kind hands like my dad, and like to build things? My dad sewed a skirt for my mother one time at the dining room table, and a dress with a pattern of autumn leaves! My dad could do these things. He built our dining room table and polished the wood until it looked like honey! My dad could cook applesauce even though we all thought it wasn't very good. Could make eggs because he'd done it in the Merchant Marines. Could read books out loud and make them real, build a fire, put up a tent, take out a splinter, do funny little dances, make us laugh.

But that summer even my dad was my enemy. They wouldn't let me leave, once they got me there. I hated my family. I missed the McCarthy campaign and the noise of the city. The distraction from how I felt inside, which was scared, alone in my room with the tall windows open to the big dark Maine night and the leaves jangling together and the darkness where all my thoughts marched through.

When I lay in my bed I could hear my parents downstairs by the fire, talking. They were guarding the door. I couldn't go anywhere. Couldn't do anything. Could only lie in bed not sleeping, worrying in the hollow dark. Worrying about what happened next. Worrying that there was something wrong with me. That made me how I was.

❧

"Let's row out to the boat," my dad told me one day. "You can help me do some jobs I've got to take care of."

I shrugged. Normally I would have been delighted. Time with my dad! Without my mother horning in! Without my sister!

But now in these sour, sad days I didn't want to be with anyone, not even him.

We walked across the field to the town dock.

He untied the skiff while I stood silently by, embarrassed because the other teenagers were watching. All around us the day was bright and colorful: the dark green line of spruce trees by the shore, the lobster boats at their moorings, the blue sky and the lavender sloping mountains of Acadia across the water.

My dad pulled on the oars.

"We're concerned about you, Martha," he told me.

I stared sullenly at the sparkly water. Didn't say a thing.

"I understand that you've experimented with drugs."

Experimented with drugs. That didn't even sound like my father! It sounded like one of those articles about *rebellious youth.* Experimented with drugs had nothing to do with what it was like to get high.

"Where'd you hear that?"

"Your sister is very concerned," my dad told me.

Concerned! That tattletale! Just like her! Goody two shoes! Just like the time she said in her big sorrowful voice to me, *I saw you from the bus smoking a cigarette. I don't even feel like I know you.* God!

"She told you that?"

"She told me that you were experimenting with drugs in New York, that people were concerned about you."

I made a disgusted sound.

"I took No Doz a couple of times and I smoked marijuana once."

My dad looked at me.

"What was it like?" he asked me.

What? He'd taken me off guard.

"I don't know," I said uncomfortably. "It was okay."

"It's dangerous," he told me. "It's illegal and it's dangerous."

But he didn't know anything.

He didn't know anything about getting high. About the long yellow pills in the film case hidden in my room. About the narrow yellow joint that Cassie brought back from California. The smell of grass. He didn't know about that feeling you got in the back of your throat when you were high. The clenched tightness of speed. The loose wobbliness of grass. The heady, dizzy, steep feeling of hash. I didn't know that much either, but I was starting to. I was starting to have this other, secret repertoire of sensation.

I didn't want to talk about it, but I wanted to tell him, too.

My dad was so cool. He liked things so much. He liked the same kinds of stories I liked. He liked the oddness of the world. He was for all the right things, and weren't all those things sort of linked together—drugs and peace and free love and civil rights and the starving Biafrans—weren't they all sort of mixed in together with long hair and sandals and flowers and garlands on your head and San Francisco and the *East Village Other*? And wouldn't it be cool to be able to talk about it with my father?

But he had that stern look too. He was my mother's husband. And he'd never understand, not in a million trillion years.

So I didn't tell him anything at all.

Instead he talked. He told me about when he was in Vietnam and all the other reporters were trying marijuana and he didn't. He told me about how they lay around and didn't do their work. Went to opium dens. I hadn't tried opium yet, but a guy in the campaign, Ron Something, had said he'd get me some. What would that be like?

We rowed out to the sailboat and we climbed aboard. It was an old sloop he rented every summer. He was teaching himself to sail out of a book.

I didn't like sailing much. I stood heavily in the boat while he puttered and gave me little jobs to do. It was all made-up stuff. I didn't care. I wanted a cigarette. I didn't want to smoke in front of him, but I couldn't wait to get back to the dock so we could walk across the field and I could cut over to the high rocky ledge by Harbor Tower where I used to go to write poems in my leather notebook but now I mostly just sat up there and smoked.

I had that weird, dizzy feeling you get when you want a cigarette. I'd started feeling that way lately. I wanted to smoke all the time. Be real skinny. Toss my head back and laugh with a cigarette in my hand. Know what to say. I'd been smoking for almost a year.

✿

One of the boys on the island said he was an artist. He came up to me one evening when I'd gone down after supper to walk to the end of the dock.

"Got a cigarette?" he asked me. He was younger than I was. I knew who he was. The one with the handsome big brother, the typical sister in her bathing suit, three golden retrievers, and a big shingly house by the shore.

"You're Henry, aren't you?"

"Yeah."

I handed him a cigarette, my matches. I used kitchen matches to light my cigarettes. I liked to flick them on the big ring I wore on my right hand. The stone was enormous. My father had brought it back from someplace for my mother.

"Nice ring," he said.

I looked at it, as if I hadn't noticed. "Yeah. It's from Denmark, I think. Amber."

I held my hand out so he could see it better.

He looked young, but he looked old, too. He smoked his cigarette like an old man, staring out at the water, squinting up his eyes a little at the setting sun.

"Do you get high?" he asked me.

"Yeah. You want to?"

I didn't know what I was thinking—get high with this boy who was a kid really, who I didn't even know. But he seemed different than the others. I'd seen him walking down the road, all by himself. Maybe he was like me. Whatever that was. Different.

"Let's go down by the boathouses," he told me. "There's this place I go."

I liked that—that he had a certain place. We walked back up the dock and then followed the path through the field and around on the rocks in front of Harbor Tower. I didn't want to go right by my parents' house so they could see me. They'd all be sitting at the table right at the front window.

"Who's Martha with?" my mother would ask.

My sister would tell her. "That's Henry Carter."

Then they'd all say something like wasn't it nice I was making friends, or else they'd wonder why I was walking with him, and be suspicious.

We found a place beside one of the empty boathouses and hunkered down in the sand.

"Next summer I'm going to use this boathouse for a studio," he told me. "I'm making sculpture."

"Yeah?"

I had a joint out, and I handed it to him.

"It's not that good," I told him. I liked the way I sounded, as if I were much older and sort of weary. I could tell he thought I was cool.

"I've got some other stuff, too," I told him. "Some speed."

"You do?"

"Yeah, I got it at this place where I was staying in New York."

I liked the way that sounded, too, like I had this mysterious life. Not like I'd swiped it from my sort-of boyfriend's parents' medicine cabinet in Westchester.

He took a hit off the joint.

"Do you do art?" he asked me.

"I like to write," I said.

"Yeah. I don't like to write," he said. "It reminds me of school. I want to do art. I want to make these really big sculptures. Out of wood. Maybe stone some day."

He looked too young to make big stone things, but I didn't say so. I could tell he was handsome, in a young way. Or he'd be handsome later on when he got older. But he'd never be like his brothers who were sort of careless and wild and raced around with their outboards in the harbor, yelling things back and forth from boat to boat.

"I thought you were like this preppie kid," I told him.

"I thought you were some kind of hippie," he answered back.

It felt easy to be with him, sitting there on the chilly sand with the sun going down and the sky changing color over the mountains.

"Sometimes I think this island is the only place that's real," he told me. "Everything else, school, you know, being home, all that bullshit in Philadelphia—it's just stuff you have to wait through to get back here. But then when I'm here, I feel like I don't belong here, either."

I knew just what he meant. I was surprised, a little, that he'd tell me this, but it felt like we were both the same.

When I got home my mother looked at me. She and my dad were sitting by the fire reading in their two chairs. "Where were you?" she asked me in her heavy way. It was dark out now.

I shrugged. "Around. I went for a walk," I told her.

"I'd like to know where you go," she said.

"We were a little worried," my dad said.

My sister looked around at me, but she didn't say anything. I could tell that she felt bad that she'd betrayed me. Partly she didn't like how I was, but partly she wanted to be friends the way we used to be. And she didn't want me to be in trouble.

"Please tell us next time you'll be out late," my mother said, with her same look which wasn't a look at all, just a blank expression.

Late? It was only like *nine-thirty.* They didn't get it at all. How I was different now. That I was used to being on my own, staying in New York, taking taxis, hanging around. I wasn't going to be like this kid anymore. That was over. They just didn't get it yet.

❦

"What do you mean I can't go back to New York?"

My mother glanced at my father.

"We'd like you to stay here for now," she told me, "with the family."

"I don't want to be with the family," I said under my breath.

"What?"

"I don't want to stay here. There's nothing to do. I want to go back to New York and help with the campaign."

"Well, we're going to take it one day at a time," my mother said. "We'll see how it goes."

God! They could do anything they wanted to me! I never should have come!

She'd tricked me. I hated my sister. She'd tricked me into coming here. *To surprise the parents,* she'd told me.

And we had surprised them. *That was the best sight,* my mother kept saying, about a million times, *when I looked up and saw you two girls coming across the field.*

Yeah, that had been nice. But I thought we were just coming for a little visit.

I didn't think we were going to have to stay.

"When can I leave?" I demanded.

"We'll see how it goes."

I was trapped. I hated them all.

✿

Maine was relentlessly lovely. The ocean was blue every single day that summer. The sky was blue. The trees against the sky—those wonderful dark green trees. I hated it all.

The sailboats. The lobster boats at their moorings. The kids I didn't know who all knew one another. The rocky goddam shore. Sand Beach where you could find sand dollars big deal. All of it. I didn't want it. I wanted to be gone.

We drove back to Washington all piled into the car together the way we always did, only now we were all too big. The car smelled hot. Our knees bumped in the backseat. I wanted a cigarette. We would never get home.

9

TEACHER ANKLES

WASHINGTON WAS HOT and disastrous. It was the middle of July. I was allowed to work at the downtown McCarthy headquarters, but now there were all kinds of rules. *Come right home after work. Tell us where you'll be.*

And they wanted me to see a shrink.

We think you ought to see someone, my mother told me.

❦

I'm standing in the living room. She's on the couch. My father's put his newspaper down. I can tell he dreads this.

"What?"

"We're concerned about you, Martha," my mother tells me. She doesn't have any expression on her face.

Concerned about me!

"Your behavior's changed. You seem so angry all the time, and you won't talk to me."

"I thought you didn't believe in psychiatrists," I tell her.

"We think it may be helpful in this case," my father says.

In this case? So I'm a case now?

I usually don't say anything when it gets like this. I just clam up and stare right back at her and wait it out, but this is kind of scary. It's so outside the kind of thing my family does. We don't believe in psychiatry. They must think there's something really wrong with me. Maybe there is. Maybe that's why I acted so weird at Palisades Park. Maybe it wasn't just the pills. Maybe it's something else—something inside me that I can't get rid of. Some dark deep root.

✪

We drove out into the flat hot heat of Maryland to some odd split-level development of white houses with flat siding and turquoise trim, attached garages. What were we doing here so far away on these black, smooth asphalt roads?

The shrink's name was Dr. Mendleblatt.

Her office was in her house, in a basementy part with small, high windows and a sliding glass door.

On her bookshelves she had these corny "Peanuts" figures with big bobbing heads on little springs.

She was fat, with dyed blonde hair.

I had nothing to say to her. I wouldn't tell her anything. I'd wait it out.

We sat in her room together, the three of us; my mother looking serious, the fat shrink, me.

"Hello, Martha," she said in a calm voice.

Kindergarten voice, I thought. The kind of voice you use for retards.

"Hi," I said, staring at my hands in my lap. Putting them this way and then that way. Twisting the ring on my finger—the one with the big amber stone.

"Do you know why you're here?"

"Not exactly," I said, still not looking up.

"Do you think you could tell me how you're feeling about being here?"

Oh God.

I didn't say anything.

"Martha. Why do you hate your mother?"

I looked at her. What a rude thing to say! My mother was sitting right there. Did she really think I was going to tell her and get in trouble and have to talk about it to my mother? That's what I *didn't* want to do. Talk with my mother. Look at her face. Have to see her.

I didn't like this lady. Didn't want to tell her anything. She wouldn't get it. I didn't even know what it was myself, how I felt. Maybe I *was* crazy. I'd get this sudden, sharp sadness, and sometimes at night I'd get scared. I'd lie there and I couldn't sleep and it seemed as if everything was marching at me—everything I'd ever done wrong; the way I looked; things I'd said—everything. I kept going over and over these things in my mind. All I wanted to do was to get away from the way I felt. Not explain it! Not think about it! Not talk about it with this loser lady psychiatrist with her Linus and her Snoopy with their bobbing, outsized heads. I didn't want to tell her anything. I'd just wait.

"Maybe you can tell me something about school."

It was summer. *God.* We didn't have school now.

It was summer. It was supposed to be easy now. But everything felt dark and scary. When I was young I used to get scared like this. Even when I was a little kid I had always felt as if I didn't belong in the world, but then I had always had my family to go back to. I had my nest. My mother who was soft and warm. My dad who was kind and held me in his arms. Even my sister who belonged beside me, riding in the backseat of our car. I had that. But now I had pushed them away from me. I had decided that I didn't want them.

It felt sometimes as if I had run out of the house—run out into the night. As if I couldn't wait to get away—escape all that cloying love and all that attention and all that closeness but now, out here, it was dark and dangerous and brambly. And no one else would take me in, would put his arms around me, hold me close.

But I didn't want to tell them that.

And I was exhausted by the enormous impossibility of anyone ever understanding anything. I was weighted down with how it was inside me. It wasn't one thing. Not boys. Not school. Not even my mother, though I wanted it to be her. It was something I couldn't even name and it had always been there. And whatever it was had to do with the way sometimes I got so scared. It had to do with a kind of hunger that I didn't understand. And what could make that feeling go away? Maybe it was sex. Maybe it was food. Maybe it had to do with cigarettes. All those things could get in the way of

that vast hunger. Food. Cigarettes. Fun. Parties. Being
stoned. Laughing. Being busy. Getting away from whatever
it was; this dead enormous weight. This big, dark pull.

But did she really think I was going to tell her anything
about it? Forget it! If I told them even half of what I felt
inside they'd think I was crazy. And I just wanted to be done.
To get out of this square, bright, fluorescent room; out into
the hot day, back into the car, windows open, top down, back
into the city, back to the house, back to my room with my
stuff and all the pictures on the walls of my room. Naked doll
lying in a bed of ivy. Picasso drawing of a nude woman playing a flute. Poster of daisies and the American flag. Eugene
McCarthy in a cobblestone courtyard. Jean Paul Belmondo.
John Lennon. I wanted to go home.

"I'd like some time alone with your mother," she told me,
finally, and I went into the waiting room and sat on an ugly
plaid couch and looked at *Readers' Digest*. The girl who sur-
vived the frigid waters. There was a drawing of her clinging
to a spar. The joke page. *A man goes into a bar with a duck under
his arm. Little Jimmy raised his hand in class.* The whole world
was pointing in the wrong direction.

❧

One night in late July there was a party for the campaign
workers at some house in Maryland. Somebody said they'd
take me. They'd take me home. I had to be home by mid-
night.

"That's cool," they told my parents. "Don't worry, we'll
get her back."

There was a pool and it was already dark. People sat around the pool smoking and talking; drinking their drinks.

I didn't drink. I thought it was disgusting. It was grown-up and dull; parental.

Some people went swimming but I didn't want to go swimming, didn't want to show people, even in the quiet dark, my slippery, naked skin.

"The water looks cold," I said when somebody asked me.

A Black man came up out of the pool. Water glistened on the black woolly cap of his hair.

"God, man," he said. "That water's cold!"

He said his poor little cock had shrunk away to nothing. We all looked at his trunks and there was only this small lumpy thing under the wet black shorts. We were supposed to look. Everybody was looking. It was supposed to be funny.

It was quiet and warm under the trees by the pool. The people who lived in the house were away. Just all these McCarthy people lying around on the chaises, going in and out of the house.

"Want to get high?" this guy named Ernie asked me, and he led the way inside.

In the dark upstairs hall he tapped on a closed door and opened it slightly and we could see two bodies piled on the bed like coats.

"Nope." Ernie shut the door. "Let's try in here," he said.

It must have been the master bedroom. It was large and wide with a huge bed. Ernie lay across it, patted the bedspread beside him.

"Come on, Martha. I won't bite."

I sat down on the bed. I didn't know him, really. He had a

brown beard. He was a little too friendly, but he wasn't scary.

But there's just something about him I don't like, someone had said.

I didn't know what it was, either, but there was just something.

Now he took out a little baggie of grass and a small pipe, and fiddled with it in an expert way. I wanted to be like that. Not avid, the way a kid would be, or making remarks about *the buds, man,* which I knew was lame. I wanted to do it the way Ernie did it—casually sticking the pipe down into the bag, pushing in the marijuana, drawing the smoke in smoothly, saying something in a tamped-down voice. He held his smoke in the whole time I sucked the sharp hot air from the pipe. I tried to hold it down myself, and started coughing, hot-faced, wet-eyed, with the smoke all fiery in my throat.

He finally let his out in a cloud of dust.

"You okay?" he asked and took the pipe from me.

I nodded, still coughing.

"Take some water," he suggested, and I went into the bathroom, cupped my hands and drank, standing over the sink, letting the cold water splash up onto my hot cheeks, drying my hands on somebody else's towel.

He was still smoking, watching me from where he lay on the bed.

"You want some more?"

I said okay and this time I could hold it down, it didn't make me cough, and then again, a few more times, and there was a knock on the door and someone opened the door and peered in, "Jesus!"—shut the door.

Ernie chuckled.

"They think we're making love in here," he said.

How could they think that? His head was that way; I was way down here by his feet. We had our clothes on. But it was dark, I thought. But he was twenty-four. Too old for me. So how could anybody think that?

"You want some more?" he asked me.

I took the pipe. The stem was unpleasantly wet from his mouth but I pretended that I didn't care.

Sucked in and held it. I could hold it easily now. I felt it, that light lifting. Everything falling away.

"You really like it, don't you?" Ernie asked.

I felt as if he were asking something different, but it didn't matter. I didn't answer him, just lay back and turned my head toward the window with the trees outside. The light—from the moon? the streetlight? swimming pool lights?—shone quietly. I could hear the party downstairs. It reminded me of a ship—as if we were on some vast ship somewhere. There was a party on another deck, but we were in some odd, far, distant stateroom, quiet and serene with quiet waves.

Ernie lit a cigarette and I could smell the warm smell of the smoke. It smelled delicious: masculine and friendly.

I reached my hand out lazily and waggled my fingers at him.

He handed me the cigarette.

"This what you want?" he asked.

I nodded, though I didn't move my head.

I smoked, lying on my back on that enormous bed that seemed to go on forever in every direction.

The smoke from the cigarette went down much easier. I pictured the kind blue smoke sailing into my body, filling up the inside of my clean, white bones. Smoke like water. Smoke like a river. Smoke like conversation. Smoke like thoughts.

I wanted to smoke forever, but reluctantly I held the cigarette out to Ernie. It was his, I argued with my selfish self.

"It's okay," he told me gently, "you can keep it."

That was so kind! He was so kind, I thought.

A whole cigarette for me!

But now there was something else. The ash dropped onto the side of my face feathery, light, warm; it did not burn me. I batted it away. But something. I had to do something about that terrible ash. Next time I might not be so lucky. I thought about it with the kind of ponderous logic you feel when you are building something out of wooden blocks; balancing the short ones on the long ones, putting the narrow, tall ones on their ends.

"Might not be so lucky," I muttered, rolling over onto my side and searching the rug with my hand in the darkness.

"What are you doing?" came Ernie's lazy voice.

I didn't know what I was doing, feeling the bumpy roughness of the carpet, hanging off the side of the slippery bedspread, cigarette raised like a torch, its red tip in the darkness. I didn't know.

I wanted something. It might be there, on the floor. I felt around. Felt something. Shoes. My shoes?

But what if I was feeling around in the dim dark and I felt a shoe and thought it was my shoe but then what if I felt some more and there was a foot in the shoe—the solidness of

EXPECTING TO FLY 🌀

toes deep in the shoe and then, as I felt my way up—ankles!
Ankles in tight nylon stockings. Teacher ankles. I would be
in trouble.

"This what you're looking for?" asked Ernie's voice.

He pulled me gently back and rolled me over. Handed me
an ashtray.

"Is this what you want?"

He knew! Knew everything about me!

I could be completely open and honest with this one. This
savior of the ashtray. This kind, bearded face in the dim darkness. This man on the bed with me, marooned on the bed, an
island in the sea of this enormous room.

I wanted to thank him but I didn't need to thank him. I
didn't need to say anything. I could just be here with him. I
could just be. *That's* what they meant by that.

He set the ashtray on the bed between us.

I laid my cigarette down carefully in the wide ceramic
dish. It was irregular. I could imagine what it might look like.
A sort of aqua blue. Very big and planey in shape. Maybe
some weird little speckles in it. Like a turquoise thing. Modern in an old-fashioned Fifties way. Modern like Formica
counters spangled with silvery gray designs. Modern like
those chairs with a certain kind of lozenge-shaped cushions.
Modern like no arms on chairs. Metal tubing. Why did *modern*—the word *modern*—seem so old?

There were all these things to think about.

There were so many explanations and complications and
innuendoes; if you said this would they think you meant
that? If you talked about *modern* would they think about sex?

Was there a connection? You didn't want that. You had to skitter back from that sharp edge. You couldn't let them see what you were thinking.

But he already knew. He had known something. The ashtray. But wasn't there something else? The shoes. The legs in the shoes. The teacher by the bed. The teacher watching. That was a little. Something. A little—don't even think it—*scary*.

The dark in the room seemed different. Darker. I could feel him there at the other side of the bed, knowing things.

"Want to go downstairs?" he asked me.

I hadn't even thought of that before. The whole other places we could go.

"Yeah," I breathed into the dim air.

He peeled himself up off the bed. It took forever. He was so tall. Walked around until he was over me.

He held his hands out. If I didn't flinch, he might not hurt me.

But he was only helping me up. Took my hands in his big, wide, cool man hands, and pulled me to my feet. We jostled against each other; his body momentarily pushing against mine. My face against the chest of his shirt. I could smell him. He put his arms around me and we stood together. It was quiet, but I could hear a buzz in the room.

He made a little noise. It wasn't words. And then he took his arms away and I rocked on my feet but didn't fall. I felt small, tall, everything.

He led the way out of the room. I came behind him. I was proud. I had remembered to pick up my shoes.

As we came down the stairs someone said something out loud.

There was a shout from the crowd below.

"Here they come!"

And someone said in a reproachful, faraway voice, "God, man, she's only sixteen!"

They thought something else had happened up there but it didn't happen and that was funny and we laughed and then they thought that meant it *did* happen and we laughed some more, almost falling against each other down the staircase, coming down into the room where people were sitting on the couches and the chairs, leaning against the tall counter in the kitchen, coming in the door or leaving. It was late, but it didn't matter. They were all my friends. They would protect me.

I sat down on the couch and Ernie came over and lay down and put his head in my lap looking up at me so that I could see his bearded face, which was familiar and unfamiliar. Which was kind and solemn. We didn't even have to talk.

Somebody walked by; the Black guy in his bathing suit.

"Man," he said, glancing at us, at Ernie with his head in my lap, and "Man, I don't believe it," in a disgusted way. He didn't look at me. It didn't matter.

I had to go home. I knew that. That was the next thing.

✿

"You're late," my mother said at the door.

I wasn't as stoned now.

My stonedness was like a wet cup of old coffee with a cig-arette floating in it. The coffee all cold now. The cigarette swollen with liquid.

I was heavy in my dress. I had my shoes in my hand.

She stood aside to let me in the door, leaned out into the night and saw Ernie standing by the car. There were other people inside the car. We had driven for a long time, it seemed like, trying to find our way back from Chevy Chase. I was no help. *It's in the second alphabet,* I'd kept saying. That's how it worked in Washington. The letter streets. The two-syllable names. The three syllables, spreading out from the center. I could think about that for a while, but meanwhile the dark roads unspooled around us and the car sped forward and then went more slowly past tall Washington houses set up on their banks of ivy and crape myrtle and their own tall, solemn trees.

Ernie raised one arm as he climbed wearily back into the car.

"Who was that?" my mother asked me in a tired voice.

She closed the door and leaned back against it, folding her arms over her chest, looking at me in the hall.

"Who was that who drove you home?" she asked.

I didn't look up at her again.

"Ernie Charmichael," I told her.

His name sounded silly, even to me. I couldn't think of anything to tell her about him—where he was from, what he did in the campaign—anything.

"Go to bed," my mother told me. "We'll talk about this in the morning."

I went up the stairs. My room was the same. In her room my sister slept soundly. Her door was open. We were supposed to leave our doors open in the summer so that the fan that my father had installed in the attic could suck the cooling air in through our windows, billowing the curtains, pulling the night air in and up through our rooms, through the house, cooling all of us as we lay under our sheets in the dark summer nights in 1968 in Washington, D.C.

IO

FORGERY IS
A CRIMINAL ACT

KIT, ONE OF THE GIRLS at school, gave me some pills.

She sat cross-legged on her dorm bed, shaking them into her hand.

"My mother takes these sometimes," she told me. "I swiped them when I was home over the summer. I think you'll like the effect."

Kit was tall and storky—a boarder from the South somewhere, or Texas. She and Sophie shared a room together, and they had it all fixed up like an apartment, with paintings on the walls and special cushions.

Sophie came into the room. "Is she corrupting you?" she asked me. "Watch out for her. She's *dangerous*."

Sophie said this last word in her breathy way. She wasn't like the rest of us. She was sophisticated. She'd done everything already. She was even sort of going bald. Her hair on top was really thin. You could see her little round scalp like the scalp of an old lady through her cloudy hair. She was short and plump like a little bird and wore wire-rimmed glasses and a wide, black straw hat with peacock feathers and a quilted velvet jacket on weekends, when she didn't have to wear her uniform. She came from Pittsburgh.

She had this way of laughing as if we were all cute, awkward puppies whereas she . . .

She'd done everything. She laughed when we said that. "Oh not *everything*," she said. "Not everything. Not *yet*."

But yes, she had.

She wouldn't ever tell you the whole story. She'd give you little glimpses, like the time going into the Schoolhouse when a cold breeze blew across the Oval and she squealed, "*Oooooooooohhhhhhhhhh*."

When I asked in my humble way, bundled in my thick coat, "What?"

She said, "It's so *chilly*. I'm not wearing any underwear."

So then, whether I wanted to or not, I had to imagine how it must be under that gray wool uniform skirt of hers. Her plump little privates. Tucked up but uncovered, like a hen or something.

She would come over on weekends and stay with one of us—the day girls. But then she'd always go off on her own.

"Let's go down to Georgetown," she'd say, and we would, but then she'd peel away from us. Later we'd meet up with her talking to Gustavo the Puerto Rican boy with the long hair who we'd heard did smack. When we came up he'd touch her cheek with the back of his hand and lope off, bouncing on his rubbery soles. He was cute but he was sort of scary. We didn't know him.

She'd look after him with a sad, motherly look.

"I'm worried about him, Martha," she would tell me.

"He's doing a little too much . . ." then she would stop as if we weren't supposed to know. She was, but we weren't.

✿

And sex. She'd done it.

We knew that.

I figured someone older. A man. Because she wasn't pretty in the little blonde way like the girls who did it regularly and talked about it in the locker room at school. There was something lost about her that I couldn't name. She fended us off with her adultness; held us away while she pretended to be our dear, dear friend. But we felt that nobody at Madeira really knew her, not even Kit, who shared her room.

"Try these," Kit suggested now, holding out some little pink pills, as Sophie watched us, with her secret smile.

"Take them both?" I asked her.

"Sure," she shrugged. "Or, I don't know, take one right away and then wait and take another one maybe in a few hours. But don't plan to operate any heavy machinery," she said. "Or drive a car."

✿

I was learning to drive.

My mother took me to the Best & Company parking lot

and we drove in slow sad circles not speaking. She pounding the phantom brake on the passenger side with her foot. Me scared and proud sitting there beside her in our shiny black, red-leather-lined Studebaker Lark, gliding over the dusty autumn asphalt in the quiet night.

I took one of the pills Wednesday morning outside the Georgetown Library, then sat on the chilly cement steps in the warm September sun and watched the school bus pull around the corner and watched the girls climb in. I was taking a day off.

I didn't really mind school as much this year. We all were seniors. We were sort of stars. In September I had given a talk to the whole school about being in Chicago—about the McCarthy campaign and the Conrad Hilton and the tear gas in Grant Park and talking to Phil Ochs. Nobody else in our school had ever done anything like that. Now when I walked around campus I felt special and important. And I was taking Creative Writing with Mrs. Libby, a teacher I really liked. She let us write cool stuff; not just boring discussions of other peoples' books, but real stories that we tore out of our hearts. Peculiar situations. Run-on sentences. Odd use of words. And I had a new friend, Mia. She came from Iowa and she was really little and she liked the same stuff I liked— writing poetry and acting silly, doing art. She'd read the books I'd read. She understood about Kerouac and Vonnegut and Jerzy Kosinski and Tom Wolfe. We could talk about serious things like God or art, but then, another minute, we would just be silly. I didn't mind getting off the bus now at the Oval because she'd be there in her little red and black lumber jacket and there was always so much to tell each other! Sometimes I noticed other girls, younger girls, looking at us with a wistful look when we came out of the senior clubhouse. They wished they could be like us, I realized— nearly grown-up, easy in our own skin. I didn't really feel that way all the time, but when they looked at me like that, I felt as if I did.

But I couldn't go to school every day. I had a certain position at Madeira now. I wasn't just some day girl. The person I'd invented was a little wild and outrageous and a little crazy, maybe. *You're so crazy, Martha!* the other girls would tell me. *God. You'll do anything!* I would.

I was skipping school. I hid my schoolbooks under a bush and then, lighter, in my school uniform and my old army jacket with the pink pill blossoming inside me and all the possibilities before me, I leapt down the long curved steps— down into the day.

It felt like spring but it was early autumn. It felt like summer but the summer was over. I felt light, feathery, sharp-boned and optimistic.

Down into Georgetown: the smell of fresh bread from the French Market; the bitter smell of coffee and the passing cars. I'd have adventures. The whole day was mine.

❧

The library on Saturday, where you worked off your demerits with detention, was a lonely place. At the end of the long

room there was a fire in the fireplace, where two green Nau-
gahyde couches sat. The heat from the fire made them smell
weird, like canned peas or something.

I'd brought my books. I might as well do my Latin homework. There was nothing else.

Outside the campus looked brown and drab—the lone
girl walking by in weekend clothes. Some teacher with a dog.
Miss Shank, the headmistress.

I saw her striding in her polo coat. She didn't see me. I
didn't want her to. Later, when nobody was looking, I'd go
downstairs and smoke cigarettes in the girls' room.

✿

She'd called me out of class on Monday morning. I was sitting next to Mia in Algebra II. The white-haired secretary
from Main Building came in, said something to the teacher,
looked at me.

"Miss Shank would like to see you in her office after class."

That's how she liked to do it.

Mia gave me a sympathetic, rueful look. She knew already.
"You're going to get in trouble," she had warned me.

"But it was worth it."

"Yeah," she said, and looked away.

✿

I sat in the satiny, striped, fancy little chair in the hall outside Miss Shank's office. She liked to make us wait.

Mrs. Fritts, the assistant head, came out, in her mint-green wool suit like a French poodle or something with her careful hair.

"Ah, Martha," she said, looking at me through her glasses. She was like the worst Madeira girl grown up—the prissiest, fanciest—the one that least understood all the stuff that my friends understood. Stuff about art and poetry and God and getting high—about the snarl and tangle of life. She didn't get anything. She was just stuck in what she was, with all her little rules and manners and her perfect little suits and her pointy glasses and her neat certainty about the world.

She stopped, in her tiny, pointy, high-heeled shoes and looked me up and down, there in my uniform with my brown oxfords like big hooves—my green Madeira sweater, my gray Madeira skirt, and then over everything the big-man herringbone wool overcoat I'd bought for fifty cents at the Christ Child Opportunity Shop. It was way too big.

Are you allowed to wear that?

I don't know. I guess I'll find out.

I would have liked her better if she'd said, "Some coat!" and snorted, but Mrs. Fritts would never snort. She just looked at me with her cold little greeny-blue eyes in the sunny hallway right outside Miss Shank's office. She knew I was in trouble. She probably knew what for. She crimped her mouth up. *Hmmmf.* And walked away.

❦

"Martha." Miss Shank's voice was like a man's voice. She stood at her office door, staring right at me with her glittery eyes.

"Come in please."

I followed reluctantly into her lair.

She went around behind her big square desk and sat down in her big chair, folded her hands on the blotter before her. There was always a box of Kleenex on the corner of her desk in case she made you cry. She usually did. I hated Miss Shank but I was afraid of her. In a certain way she reminded me of my mother but a really mean, scary, nightmare version of my mother. Even though I knew she wouldn't really hit me, I felt like she might hit me. Her office was scary. It was dark and full of dark wood and even the outside looked different though her windows—the grass less green, the trees all dim and stern.

"Tell me where you were yesterday."

"I was in Georgetown."

She closed her eyes for a moment as if to contain her rage. "In *Georgetown?*"

"I skipped school."

She looked for a moment. She could do anything. She might start yelling or just sit there staring at me with her scary stare. Or she might talk in her quiet voice. That's what she did.

"You skipped school," she repeated. "And what did you imagine would happen? That no one would notice?"

"I don't know."

"You *don't know.*"

She stared at me.

"Well, what did you intend to do about an excuse?"

"I don't know."

"I believe it is *customary* for our day students to provide a note from their parents when they are absent."

I didn't say anything. I'd called. I'd called from a pay phone outside People's Drug Store on Wisconsin Avenue and told them I wasn't coming in, that I was sick. I hadn't thought about what I would do for a note. I could never imitate my mother's handwriting. Her big square words.

"So, Martha, tell me: Would you have *forged* a note?"

I shrugged.

"Because if you had," she went on, ignoring me, "I would have been forced to dismiss you. We do not tolerate felony in this school."

Felony?

"Forgery is a *criminal act.*"

Now I almost did laugh, but it wouldn't have been a good laugh. It would have been a weak, nervous kind of laugh. Worse, in a way, than crying. And I didn't want to give her that.

She was probably going to tell me I had all this detention time. Saturdays in the library blah blah blah. But she surprised me.

"Martha," she said, still in that mean, sarcastic way of hers, like she knew all these things about you that you didn't want anybody to know. "You're a very talented girl. And, I believe, a bright one. You are also charismatic. You have the ability to be a leader here, and yet you have chosen to be a rebel. I think you might want to reconsider your path."

Was she complimenting me or threatening me? Even when she said something she meant to be nice, it sounded mean. *Charismatic.* Like President Kennedy, and look what happened to him.

"That will be all," she told me. "You'll serve detention for four consecutive Saturdays. I trust this episode won't be repeated."

✿

I trust this episode won't be repeated, I said to myself now in the bathroom in the basement of the library. I was smoking a cigarette, blowing the smoke upward at the ceiling ventilation duct. I hadn't smoked in so long that it made me feel dizzy. Almost like getting high, I thought. And when I walked back up into the library I felt light, taller, more unusual.

Later that afternoon I was walking home from Wisconsin Avenue when somebody called my name.

"Martha!"

There were a bunch of them sitting just inside the fence at Rosedale. Brendan and his brother and sister. Braxton Theobald. A couple of others. Most of them were younger than I was. They lived in my neighborhood, but they went to Hawthorne, the hippie school. Molly was wearing a long black cloak. She had long black hair. She was only about thirteen but she already got high all the time. She had beautiful eyes.

"Come on!"

They had a joint.

"Want to go in the boxwoods?" they asked me.

"Sure." I shrugged.

It felt funny, getting high in the boxwoods. They were so big they were like little rooms inside, with the damp earth and the strange spicy smell of the leaves. I used to play there all the time when I was little. We'd make up stories and pretend the different bushes were different rooms. Now we crouched together on the damp dirt passing a joint back and forth. Smoking cigarettes and stubbing the butts out in the ground. I couldn't tell if it was cool to be doing this or some sort of sacrilege. Or maybe it was both.

"You okay?" Brendan asked me.

He was almost as old as me. He was nice.

♦

My parents were standing outside the schoolhouse when I came out a few days later. The air was chilly.

"What's wrong?"

"We need to talk to you," my mother told me.

She was wearing her big coat. My dad in his suit with his bow tie and his overcoat. It was cold out.

Maybe somebody had died; they had to tell me.

I got into the back seat and we drove out through the gate and down the road the wrong direction—not back toward Washington—but out in the other direction, out into the country of Virginia, beyond McClean.

"Where are we going?"

"We thought we'd go out to Great Falls."

Great Falls?

We used to go there when we were little. We would take a picnic and explore on the rocks. *Don't get too close, girls!* The water was dangerous. You could stand up high and look down at the tumbly waves crashing over the rocks below.

Then we'd go on the merry-go-round. Annie on the brown horse. I'd take the black.

It was all shut up now, for the winter. The parking lot was empty. It was cold.

We walked together along the path down toward the water. The big old-fashioned house where you could get hot dogs and popcorn, stuff like that, was shuttered now and silent. Its big porch empty. Nobody anywhere around.

The merry-go-round looked weird with the cover over it. Boarded up. You couldn't see the horses.

When we got to the picnic tables near the rocks, and my parents still hadn't told me anything, I started to get this scary feeling. Had they brought me here to kill me? Were they going to throw me over the rocks into the boiling water of the Potomac? Nobody around. The silent picnic tables.

We don't know where she is. She disappeared.

But when we sat down, my father said, "We're worried about you, Martha."

"What?"

"Your mother found some things you'd written in your room."

"You went in my room?"

"I had to know what was going on with you," my mother said. "You won't talk to me anymore."

Her face looked soft and sad, but she'd looked in my room. *What had she looked at? Read my diary? Poked around in my stuff?*

"What did you read?"

"A note or something, I don't know. You said you were smoking dope. Are you?"

Oh God.

"No."

I couldn't look at them. They were so stupid.

"Are you, Martha?"

"No! I told you."

"Then what?"

"I don't know, I just wanted to be cool. I wrote that. It was like a story or something."

"We're very concerned," my father told me in his other voice.

"So what do I have to do? Go back to the shrink again?"

"No," my mother said that word like it was this big heavy thing she had to lift and didn't have the strength for. "No, that didn't work. I don't know what to do, Martha. We just want you to finish school successfully. Do your work."

Mmmm hmmmm. They weren't going to kill me. I just had to wait this out, and we'd go home.

🌀

"Maybe you shouldn't go to college," my mother told me.

We were driving in the car, a few days later.

"I'm not sure school is for you."

But then what? Everybody I knew went to college.

"I'm thinking about Antioch or Bard," I said.

"Yes, that might work."

But she said it in this vague way—as if my future were some dark, foggy, disappointing place, where she couldn't travel.

II

BATHING BEAUTY

"JEFF?"

"Yeah."

"It's Martha."

"Oh. Hi."

"I got your letter."

"Yeah."

"I'm coming to New York."

"You are?"

"Yeah, with my father. We're meeting my sister there. She goes to Smith now. We're going to a McCarthy reunion party. Are you going? It's at Doris Perleman's."

"No, I didn't know about it."

"You can still go, if you want to."

"When are you coming?"

"Next weekend. We're going to the party Saturday night

and then on Sunday afternoon my father and I are going to Bard. I have an interview."

"You want to go there?"

"I don't know. It looks okay. I thought maybe I could see you."

"Yeah, okay. Where are you staying?"

Jeff met me at the hotel. I hadn't seen him since the summer. He looked the same only now he was wearing a leather jacket. We'd written to each other and talked on the phone a couple of times, but it was different; seeing him in person. He looked kind of short.

In Central Park we sat together by a pond and he put his arms around me the way we used to sit sometimes last summer. He told me he had headaches all the time now. Stress. He was talking to his father about it because—didn't I remember?—his father was a psychiatrist.

"I know. I used to take drugs out of your parents' medicine cabinet. Those yellow pills. I might even still have some."

He moved away from me a little.

"My dad thought you must have some sort of a problem," he told me. "How you were always crying. I told him about it."

He told his *father* about me?

I tried to act like it didn't matter.

"What did he say?"

"That's what he said. I just told you. That you must have some sort of a problem."

He shifted. I felt big in his arms. *Was I fat now?* It was cold and the ground was hard. He was different than last summer. Smaller.

"Do you want to go to the McCarthy reunion party tonight?" I asked him.

"No. I'm done with all that political stuff. I'm taking business courses."

Business courses?

"When I get finished at NYU, I want to get a good job. Maybe in advertising. You can make good money."

"Yeah. So when will I see you? I have to go back tomorrow afternoon."

"I'll see you in the morning. I'll pick you up early at your hotel. We'll go someplace."

✦

I thought about seeing Jeff in the morning. I decided I'd do anything. Anything he wanted. With his headaches. With his business courses. Maybe I was in love with him. Maybe this was what love felt like. Sort of sharp and achy. Like the center of something. Everything seemed to have something to do with last summer. The Park and how it looked. The buildings. Where we'd gone. I'd been too young then; hadn't understood. That night in his brother's bedroom.

But I knew more now. I was different. Maybe he could be in love with me.

Early in the morning he was in the lobby sitting in a chair wearing his leather jacket. He looked handsome, and when he was sitting down you couldn't tell that he wasn't very tall. He looked like a man, with his curly hair and his beautiful gray eyes and he had a newspaper like a man would have a newspaper and sit in a hotel lobby waiting for a woman to come down.

When I came into the lobby I looked right at him, and I felt light and bright and perfect in my skin. It was early. I had hardly slept at all. My sister was still asleep in the other bed in our room. My father in his room still sleeping. I had told them I was going out for breakfast. It was Sunday morning. It was five A.M.

"Oh, Martha," Jeff said, looking up.

He didn't smile or anything. Just got up from the chair and took my hand, but I was glad to be with him, excited to be going out into the mysterious early streets of New York City; to be walking down the street with him at last. *This is what it feels like,* I thought.

"Where are we going?"

Maybe we would just walk around like people in a movie, talking and laughing, holding hands. Doing wacky things like they did in movies—people who were in love.

"Let's go to my father's office. It's right near here. I've got the key."

So we didn't walk around, after all, we just walked a few blocks. Then we came to a tall, serious building. We went into the old-fashioned lobby and took a small, brown elevator to the seventh floor.

His father's suite was like a dentist's office with magazines. It felt weird to go through the waiting room without waiting, like going backstage at an empty theatre.

His father's office was dark and serious too. The desk was broad and had a big, dark, rose-colored blotter with leather corners. There were big shelves of books and there was a long couch with dark rose-colored fabric and a design of little diamonds.

Jeff pulled me down onto the couch.

I liked it. I liked being in this mysterious place—his father's psychiatry office. Lying down on the psychiatrist couch where the crazy people lay and talked about themselves. It would be funny, later, a funny story that I told my friends.

But right now it wasn't all that comfortable. The narrow couch wasn't designed for two people, one of them a big young girl in an awkward dress and a poncho.

"Let's take that off," Jeff said, and he pulled it over my head.

He lay down beside me with his arms around me and I felt the weird flesh of his leather jacket against my face.

"Here," he said, sitting up again, taking off his jacket and throwing it onto the floor.

I had already decided I would let him do it. Everybody else had done it, it turned out, over the summer, when I wasn't looking. Cassie had done it. I was pretty sure Sydney Jane had done it. The girls in the locker room. Even some of my sister's friends had done it. Everybody except for me.

But now that we were here, on the psychiatrist couch with the little diamonds and the bulgy hard part of the couch where you put your head, I didn't feel sexy at all. I didn't feel the way people felt or said they felt in books: swept up in a spiral of passion, rushed along by a furious flow. I didn't feel all melty and smooth the way I'd sometimes felt when we were kissing in his parents' basement. I felt awkward and gritty. It was too early in the morning and the room around us was too big and serious and dark.

But then his face was on mine and I closed my eyes so I wouldn't have to see it get larger and darker, and then, as he rolled toward me, there were his lips and the familiar cave of his mouth and the taste of toothpaste and the smell of him which now I remembered—a wonderful smell which had to do with leather and some kind of perfumey soap and, under all those smells, the smell that was only his.

We kissed for a long time and his hands moved around and undid the back of my dress and he pulled the dress down and he was touching my breasts and putting his mouth to them the way men did and sucking on them which kind of hurt but was also exciting. And it was exciting to see my own breasts in the dim light of the office and his face bent over them serious and entranced.

He put his hand up under the skirt of my dress and he touched me and I would have done anything, then. Anything to keep his hand there touching me. And I no longer felt the couch or anything, just the center of feeling that was where his hand was, where his mouth was.

There was nobody there. I closed my eyes against the

strange dimness of the room and I lay back and waited for everything to happen.

He didn't say anything.

I could hear the sound of his mouth on my breast and the sounds of our bodies moving on the narrow couch. And I could hear the sounds of the city far away and below as the day came into life around us. *This is it,* I kept thinking. *This is how it is.*

But then he rolled over on top of me. He was heavy and he pushed himself against me, pushed hard so that his rough jeans rubbed against me hard and rough and it hurt. I tried to get loose from him, but he was all on top of me, pushing against me, holding me down by my shoulders, and I couldn't understand, as I looked at the mask of his face, why he hadn't just taken our clothes off, because I would have let him, and he didn't need to do this angry secret thing—this rubbing and scraping against me that didn't feel wonderful the way his hands had felt wonderful, that didn't feel soft and magical, but felt hard and angry and mean. He rubbed harder and faster and harder and then his whole body stiffened against me and he made an angry, mean gasp of a sound and fell down on me, heavy as a corpse, and I waited until he rolled off and stood up and he spoke.

All he said was, "Let's go."

He left me lying there and went into the bathroom. I could hear the water. When he came out the front of his jeans was wet, but I tried not to look.

He didn't say anything.

It was like we had done some terrible thing together and we weren't supposed to talk about it. But we hadn't done anything, not really. We'd just done what we'd always done. But this time it felt terrible and final.

He didn't stroke my hair or take my hand, or smile or say, *I've really missed you.* I wanted him to do all of those things, or even just one of those things, but he didn't.

We walked back through the streets in shamed silence. I felt rumpled and bruised in my clothes.

When we got back to the hotel he stood apart from me and he said, "Well, I guess I'll see you," and I didn't know what I was supposed to say, so I just said, "Yeah," and then he kind of leaned over and kissed me on the cheek like you'd kiss an old aunt or something and he left.

I went up to the room and my father and my sister were waiting for me.

"We've been waiting," they told me. "What took you so long?"

❧

On the plane back to Washington I started crying.

My father looked at me with his serious face.

"What's the matter?"

"I don't want to go to Bard. I can't go there," I told him.

We'd visited the college in the afternoon. I'd felt like an alien there—sour and tired from the morning and too little sleep. The campus was shabby and sad; everything reminded me of Jeff. I didn't tell my dad all that, of course. I just said I didn't like the college. That I didn't want to go there.

"Then you won't," he said. "If you don't like it, don't go."

That was how it was with my dad. It was simple.

✿

I went back to New York a few weeks later by myself. I thought I could see Jeff again and maybe this time I could get rid of my virginity once and for all. It was colder now, the middle of November, and the streets were desolate.

I called Jeff from a pay phone outside the public library. Little bits and pieces of crud blew down the street and got into my eyes, and I turned my back to the wind and held the cold hard phone close to my ear.

"Yes?" his mother answered the phone. I could imagine their little white house out in Westchester.

"Is Jeff there?" I asked her. I didn't want to tell her who I was. *I don't think it's a good idea for girls to call boys.*

He was there. He got on the phone.

"Yeah?"

"It's Martha," I told him.

"Oh, hi," he said.

"I'm here," I told him.

"Where?"

"Here. In New York City. I'm right outside the library. You know, where we went that time?"

There was a silence. I didn't like how it sounded.

"So, what are you doing?" he asked me.

"Talking to you," I said.

It was meant to sound vivacious, but it sounded stupid. I felt really stupid, standing there freezing to death in the sharp wind. Stupid in my clothes; short and stumpy. Standing by the pay phone with the hard phone pressed to my ear. His voice sounded tiny in the black receiver. Tiny and faraway. He sounded like a mean photograph of a man. I couldn't even remember exactly what he looked like. Could only picture a sort of snapshot image in which his head was turned away. I could see his sideburn, his ear and part of his jaw, the curly brown back of his head, his shoulder.

"I thought that while I was here we could maybe get together."

"Oh."

"I mean, I've got a ton of things to do," I said. "I just thought I'd call and see."

"Well, I don't know. I'm out here. I mean, how long are you staying?"

"Just until tomorrow. I have to go back. School." I said it like he'd know I didn't belong there, how I was really this person who could travel to New York or anywhere, take taxis, anything, fly off in planes.

"Oh. I really. I guess I can't," he said. "Look, I mean you didn't even let me know that you were coming. And I'm sort of seeing somebody now. This girl at school. She's more my type I guess. And you know, you aren't exactly a bathing beauty."

Those were his exact words. *Bathing beauty.* Whatever that meant. What I wasn't. Twin girls in matching turquoise bathing suits with legs tucked under sitting by a pool where later in the evening pairs of girls with matching swim caps would perform synchronized events all up and down the long bright pool, coppery and pleasant in the fading light.

"Okay," I said. What else could I say? He was seeing somebody. A bathing beauty. Which I would never be. Of course I already knew I wasn't pretty, but to be *told* that, over the phone, standing in the harsh November wind in New York City with the dirty sidewalk and the tall, blank, uncompromising faces of the buildings.

"Okay," I said. "Well, I guess I'll see you."

I hung up. I didn't want to hear him say good-bye.

I walked back into the library. The dark wood tables and the dark wood chairs. The books and bums and marble floors.

I kept thinking the words over and over—*bathing beauty. You're not exactly a. Seeing somebody. This girl from school.*

I could picture her. With her perfect skin and her flawless, flipped-up hair and her little feet in little shoes and her makeup and her bag. All of it. All of it completely different from me.

I called Doris, a woman that I knew from the campaign.

"Oh Martha," she said when I told her. "That bastard! I remember when Brad Buckminster said something like that to me in the fourth grade. He said I looked like a witch. It was the meanest thing. But don't listen to him. You're beautiful. He just doesn't know anything. That's all.

"And anyway," she said, "is he really so great?"

I didn't know. Did it even matter? Wasn't what mattered if he loved me? If anyone loved me at all—even a little bit— I would love him right back.

I2

WRESTLING IN THE DARK

IN FEBRUARY Langston Hughes came to our school. He was going to do a reading and then there was a special reception at Main Building. Only seniors could go.

My friends and I couldn't wait to meet him. We all wanted to be poets. Rebel poets. Some of the other girls wrote poetry—like Myra Limpet with her pale ashen skin and black, lank, greasy hair. She read Emily Dickinson and got good grades and had these long, earnest discussions about *cadence* and *metaphor* with Miss Spencer. We were different. Cassie, Sydney Jane, Mia, Dianna, and I. We wrote poems that were like yells. Poems you were supposed to shout out loud. We did shout them out loud. Some of our poems didn't make sense but that was how they were supposed to be. Nothing made any sense. That was the whole point.

He was a little disappointing when he stood up to give his reading in the gym. He looked like a businessman or something with his kind, round brown face and his careful way of talking. He was kind of old. But it was really cool to hear him read his poems. I'd read them and had them read to me in Miss Treakle's horrible screechy voice as she walked across the front of the room with loud shoes in the quiet classroom. But when he read his poems they were real. I closed my eyes so I could only hear the words and not have to see all the girls sitting around me, and then I sort of scrinched up my eyes so everything was blurry and the poet looked like a painted poet standing at a painted podium.

Afterwards, when we'd walked across the chilly campus to Main Building and stood in clumps in our uniforms and ate the brownies, drank the bitter tea, everybody was too shy to talk to him. I wondered what he thought of us. We were all so white except the two Black girls who were thrust forward at him for his approval. This prissy girls' school out in the country with the horses and hockey fields, the brick and the ivy. He probably thought we were all rich.

Mia and I went to the other side of the room and ate cookies.

But this was our big chance to meet a real writer, a poet. It was one of those times when you just have to do something.

I went up to him.

"Hi," I said.

"Hi," he said and smiled at me.

"I want to be a writer," I blurted at him. "How should I do it?"

"Write. Just write," he told me. "Just one word after another. Write it down." I said thank you and I turned away, holding his words in my hand as if they were special magic stones. I wanted to leave right then; and take the stones with me, but when I went outside into the sharp air and thought again what he had said to me, I couldn't tell if he'd told me this big important profound truth, or nothing really, nothing at all.

But I knew I'd felt something—listening to his poems, hearing him tell me to just write—some kind of understanding. Something I had always wanted and I couldn't name. I was just at the edge of it.

I knew there was something. Something beyond the boring plod of everyday. Something that had to do with God and poetry and love and peace and all the rest of it. But how were you supposed to get it? How were you supposed to name the stuff inside?

"Do you ever think about writing?" I asked Brendan. We were sitting in the grass at Rosedale, leaning against the fence, smoking a joint.

"What do you mean, writing?"

"You know, like poetry and stuff, or stories?"

"Sure," he said.

"I mean do you think you would ever do it, like for your life?"

"I don't know. I do it sometimes."

"Do you think you have to be a certain way to write? To be real intense about it? How do you think people do it? I mean write real stuff, the kind that just cuts through everything?"

I knew what I meant. I couldn't say it right. I felt like if I could tell him about how it felt inside when I thought about writing, how it felt when I read something really true, that we'd have this final kind of connection, that he'd really get me.

But, "I don't know," he said. And that was all.

✧

Brendan lived in the house around the corner. His family was Catholic. They had tons of kids. Five of them, or seven.

He had the whole third floor. It was pretty cool. His closest sister and brother, who were practically the same age, lived in the rooms downstairs, but we all hung out in Brendan's room where you could smoke.

There was a little triangular window that showed a patch of sky and branches; pillows on the floor and wooden liquor boxes for tables. We burned candles and incense and we could smoke pot up there and listen to music: Cream, Country Joe and the Fish, Canned Heat, and other stuff.

✧

We were stoned. The air was blue with parallel planes of smoke, and it was warm and peaceful.

Brendan was lying on his mattress in the shabby back part of the attic where he slept. He called me in there.

He was a year younger than I was, so nothing was going to happen. We were just friends. But there was something about him. His sulky look. His milky skin. The way his jeans fit and his long brown hair.

My mother hated him.

When he came over and sat on the eagle couch in the living room my mother would say afterwards, "My, that boy has a terrible odor."

He didn't use deodorant. He smoked. He had done acid. He'd had sex.

"Martha!"

He called me in where it was dim and secret; that room beyond the room where we hung out.

I went in. "What?"

He was lying on his mattress, said he was depressed.

I sat beside him, and he pulled me down.

"Come over here," he said.

In the other room the music kept on playing. The door was half shut. We could only see pieces of the others; part of Molly's leg, the back of Michael's head. We could hear their quiet voices from time to time. They were all pretty stoned.

We'd done this before, lay down together. We liked to pretend to fight, to struggle against each other. He was so strong. Stronger than you'd think; the way he knotted his arms and grabbed my wrists and held me down on the mattress that smelled foreign and familiar all at once.

I loved it, but I wrestled against him, pushing like I wanted to get free. This felt real. I didn't know what we were doing, but I loved it. We were struggling over something, pressing against each other. He tried to tickle me. I grabbed his hands and pushed them away. Then he got my wrists again so I couldn't move, and he leaned over me, staring down. In the darkness I could only see the shape of his head, the long hair hanging down like feathers, and the side of his face lit by the meager light from the half open door.

"I've got you," he told me. But his voice spoiled it. It was too soft, too tentative.

In the dark, with his strong arms, he'd felt just like a man.

13

INTO THE BRIGHT NIGHT

"So who is this guy?" Mia asked me. "Is he cute?"

I didn't know if he was cute. I was getting used to his face.
His hair was long and soft and it was the same color as mine.
I wanted to be around him, but then, when I was with him,
he was kind of annoying. It was like there was this other
room just beyond the room where we struggled in the dark
and he held my wrists. Just beyond the room where we
talked and got stoned and smoked cigarettes and listened to
music. There was this further place where we would be the
same people but different people; where we would touch each
other in a way that was blind and ancient. That was holy in
some way I couldn't name.

If you tried to talk about it, then it seemed normal and
cheesy like a drugstore counter.

Like Mia telling me how she and Doug had done it and they didn't have any douche and they hadn't used a rubber so afterwards he shook up a bottle of strawberry soda pop and sprayed it up into her vagina.

Gross!

I know!

Did it work?

After the magic of it and the secrecy and the hushed scariness and the oblivion—then you turned it into something else by talking with your friends.

It was how things worked. Was that what everybody was talking about in their songs and books? Was the whole world really about sex? Was every reference somehow a reference to *doing it?*

It seemed as though it were.

My skin felt too alive. My skin felt as if I had a rash or something just under the surface; as if each little hair on my arms were standing on end. As if everyone knew how I looked with my clothes off.

It was all about sex; everything. The songs and the way people dressed and how nobody wore bras anymore. I didn't wear bras anymore. You could see everybody's whole interesting breasts and their bare skin through their see-through blouses and it was okay! It was the way things were now.

Only the grown-ups were still dressed in big, stuffy clothes and the young Republicans, who were like grown-ups themselves, and the girls at my school and the friends of my parents. They all still wore their layers of girdles and bras and slips and garter belts and had their hair done in shapes, not wild and free and just however it went, but tamed and coiffed and shellacked into helmets and hairdos the way I used to before I knew!

God, we'd say, *remember how we set our hair? We put that gel in our hair to make it go a certain way? We taped the curls to our cheeks to make them go forward in two c's, one on either side, and then you got that rash on your cheeks from the Scotch tape? Yeah! I know!*

It had nothing to do with . . .

This. Staring into Brendan's flat blue eyes knowing what I knew. Knowing what was beyond knowing.

"Want to do some acid sometime?" he asked me. "I could get some."

That was the door.

❧

There was a party at Braxton Theobold's who was rich. His parents were out of town. It was cold. February. It had gotten easier to sneak out.

I'd been out already. I'd gotten stoned with Brendan walking around. There was some lame thing at American University with a light show. We walked back down Massachusetts Avenue, by the round synagogue and past the Giant Food Store, People's Drug Store, back down Newark Street. It was always down Newark Street. It was always the same— the big tall house of Peter Richardson with his black light in the third floor window. The big brick house across the street where the man who was *a little odd* lived with his mother. He was too old to live with his mother, but they were very rich and gave a big party every year on Boxing Day with fancy cookies. Past the dark jungle of Rosedale. Back toward home.

The lights were still on at the Moores' house across the street.

"I'll meet you in an hour," I told Brendan.

"Will you be able to get out?"

"Sure," I said.

We didn't kiss. We only kissed when we were making out. It still felt strange to me; his downy face. He was a whole year younger. I felt a little ashamed of being with him. But then I would think of his skin.

The house is quiet and dead inside when I come in. My parents are in the living room with all their newspapers the way they always are. "We were just about to go up," they tell me.

"You're late," my mother says. "I told you to be in by eleven."

I look at her. I don't say anything. I hate it that she gets to say that to me.

"Well?" she says, staring at me. She's on the couch. My father's in his chair.

"I'm sorry," I mutter. Inside I am having an entirely different conversation. *Bitch. I hate you.*

"Have you done your schoolwork?"

"It's Friday night," I tell her. *She's so dumb.*

"Well, I think you're falling behind," she says.

Behind what? I hate you.

"I'll work on it tomorrow."

She gives a short huff of a sigh. Like I'm way too much. "Go on up," she says, like I'm a dog.

I go up quick. I hate her. I'm never going to talk to her. Never going to tell her anything. She doesn't know anything.

I'm stoned, Mom, stoned I want to say to her. *I'm completely wrecked. How do you like that,* Mother? *How do you like me now?*

I go up to my room. I'm glad I'm sneaking out. I'm furious with her. She always gets to be in charge of me. She doesn't know anything.

I hear her come up the stairs and pass my door. I hate the way she walks. She stands for a moment right outside my door. I can practically hear her breathing. She would like, I bet she would just *love* to come in and sit on the side of my bed and have some big conversation. I don't want to talk to her. I don't even want to be around her. As soon as I can, I'm getting out of here. I'm going to leave and never come back.

And then I'll do whatever I want. I'll get stoned every day if I want to. I'll go to parties. I'll have an apartment. I won't do schoolwork or anything like that. I'll do cool stuff. I'll have cool friends. I'll have a car.

I can hear her out there, and then she moves away.

❧

It feels like the whole house is breathing. I lie in my bed with all my clothes on. When I'm sure it's safe I get up, go down the stairs and out the front door, out of that tomb of a house, into the bright night; the chilly air, the sidewalk. Brendan's waiting for me at the corner. All the houses in our neighborhood are dark.

"Did you have any trouble getting out?"

"No," I tell him. We start up the road.

I want to walk up Thirty-fourth Place and then up the backside of Rosedale on Ordway. There's a path there. It makes me think that I live in the country. The houses on the other side are quiet. They're dark brick with white trim and the windows are all blank and silent in the night.

At the corner of Thirty-fifth and Ordway there's a huge tree with branches that start low to the ground. Annie and I used to get inside of it when we were little and pretend it was our house. One time we were playing in it and an old lady came along and she smiled at us and said that she used to play in it when she was a little girl and she used to put wild daisies on her dolls' plates and pretend that they were eggs. We stared at her, and then she went away.

Tonight I want to tell Brendan about that lady. I want to take him into the tree with me and show him how we used to play there. It would be okay because we're still a little stoned; could be like a thing you do when you're stoned.

"See that tree?" I tell him.

"Yeah," he says in his light voice.

"I used to play in it."

"Oh yeah?"

He can't imagine my life.

"Come on," I tell him, and we go across the dark grass and I show him how you can step up into the tree and in the darkness the bark is cold and rough and hard. We lean back and we light cigarettes and we smoke in there, in the big tree where I used to play, leaning against the branches. And it feels weird to be there smoking cigarettes with this boy who is sort of my boyfriend, even though he's a whole year younger, in the night when my parents think that I'm in bed.

"Come on," he tells me. "Let's go to Braxton's."

Braxton lives over by Hearst, near Sidwell Friends. His parents are really rich. He's kind of weird. He's younger than most of us, and he's really small for his age; he looks about eight or something, but he takes more drugs than anyone I know and because he's so rich he's been all over—London and Paris and everywhere, Mexico and stuff. He always has drugs. And he has a great stereo system and tonight, because his parents are out of town for the weekend, the whole house is like this huge party. Upstairs and downstairs. Brendan and I are older than a lot of the other kids, so we have to act a certain way. Kind of mysterious. I can tell some of the little kids are excited that we're there. When we come in everybody's sitting around in the living room. It's the middle of the night. How did they get out of their houses? Did they all sneak out? Don't their parents wonder where they are?

They're all wrecked. Some of them look really young.

Brendan's sister and brother are there. They look up *hi, man* when they see us and then sort of lose track and stare straight forward listening to the music.

"Want to go upstairs?" Brendan asks me.

We go up the white carpeted stairs. I can hear Braxton laughing really high and crazy-sounding from the back of the house. Maybe the kitchen.

The upstairs is full of weird art. There are lights on everywhere and kids all over. Some of them are watching television in the big bedroom which I guess is the parents' room with enormous bedside lamps.

We find a room with nobody in it and we go in and smoke a joint and then we smoke cigarettes and somebody else comes in and sits down on the bed with us and we talk about stuff. We can hear the music coming up from downstairs and then the television from the other room. It's like this big club or something with everybody there.

All of a sudden Molly runs up the stairs. "Martha! Your parents!"

"What?"

"Your parents are downstairs."

"You're kidding me."

"No, they are."

I look at Brendan like he's going to fix it.

"You better go down," he says.

I get up off the bed, put out my cigarette because I've never smoked a cigarette in front of my parents. I still have my coat on. I look at Brendan again.

"I'm going down," I say.

He nods, but doesn't move off the bed, just stares at me.

I guess it's better if he doesn't come. They already can't stand him. I go down. There they are, right at the foot of the stairs, looking up. My parents in their winter coats.

"Where were you?" my mother asks me, which is kind of dumb.

"Come on," my dad says. "Let's go home."

We go outside without speaking. I look around from the doorway. Everybody looks scared and young and the whole place smells like grass. Can't my parents smell it? The music's off. Braxton is standing right by the door. It's odd; he's like this gentleman, even though he's so young and so little and everything. He says good-bye to me like his parents probably say good-bye to their guests at their parties.

I give him a sort of grimace and say, "Sorry," and he smiles at me like it's okay. Like he's telling me to be brave or something. Like he gets it. He's not what I thought he was like.

I get into the backseat. It feels so cold in there.

"How did you get here?" my mother asks me.

"I walked."

"Alone?"

"No."

I'm exhausted by what's to come. They'll yell at me and they'll ground me or something and we'll have to have this big discussion and maybe I'll be hauled back to the psychiatrist. It's all just dumb. I'm just waiting for it to be over. I just want to get out from under them but now it's like I'm starting all over again and they're still in charge and I'm going to have to listen to them yell.

Only it's not the way I imagine it. They're very quiet. Even my mother. Quiet. She only says, "We were worried, Martha. I went into your room to check on you and you weren't there. We were so worried."

And her voice sounds weird.

Maybe she's waiting until we get home. But when we pull up in front of our house she just gets out of the car and starts up the walk. That's when I see that she's put her coat on over her nightgown and it's sticking down. And on the back of it there's this dark smear of blood. She came in such a hurry.

14

SPRING

ALL OF A SUDDEN it gets warm, the way it can in Washington in the middle of March. The air changes. On a long, sleepy afternoon after classes Mia and I hang out in the Oval, lying on the grass for the first time since fall. We're seniors. We can do whatever we want. Younger girls go by on the brick paths and I know what they're thinking—how lucky we are to be seniors—how grown-up and experienced and nonchalant. I lie down on my back and stare at the branches that stick up into the sky.

"I'm taking acid this weekend," I tell Mia.

"Oh yeah?"

She doesn't entirely approve, but she would never tell me not to. She gets how I am. How I have to do these things.

"Don't you sort of feel like we own the school now?"

She looks at me with her odd, light Midwestern eyes.

"I know what you mean," she says. "Just don't let anybody hear you say that."

We have secrets together. We don't even have to say sometimes what they are. I've never had a friend like her before.

"You going home for spring break?"

"Yah," she says in her weird, flat, Iowa accent. "My parents are pretty much getting a divorce."

"Are you sad?"

She shrugs. She doesn't want to talk about it. It's okay. I don't want to either. Our friendship has nothing to do with parents. It doesn't even have to do with the school, really. It has to do with words and with stuff that's just weird and funny and this level we connect on. We can just talk and the other one always gets it.

"Want to walk around?"

"Yah, okay, sure."

We start up the steep hill toward the place where you can look out at the Potomac. The campus is pretty big.

"You know it's even kind of beautiful," I tell her. I'd only say that to her. Now that I know I'm leaving in only three more months. I'll be going to Antioch College next year if I get in. Now that I know that, Madeira seems somehow dear to me, miniature and darling. And I love being a senior. We get to hang out in the senior clubhouse. We get to have Special Privileges. The other girls sort of look up to us. All that stuff. It's not so bad. I can see why . . .

Mia doesn't hate it as much as I do.

"Well, sure," she says. "It's really beautiful."

Then it's like there's this sad, solemn feeling to the afternoon and I can't stand feeling it all—the web of our friendship, the story I'm working on for Creative Writing boiling around inside me, the achy feeling from being with Brendan, the expectation of the acid—all of it—it's too much and I just let loose and I start running up the hill and she runs along after me. She's so little that she has to run hard to keep up, and we run right to the top and we fall over laughing on last fall's old leaves and we're laughing like crazy—not with any words or explanations just crazy—I don't know—because it's so warm finally, and it's spring, and we're friends.

"Girls."

It's Mrs. Libby. We both like her. She's our Creative Writing teacher.

We roll over, look up at her. "Hi."

"Girls," she says again. She's really nice. She hardly even seems like a teacher. She loves the way we write.

"I'm glad I ran into you," she says. "Are you walking down?"

"Oh, yeah! God!" I say. I look at my watch. "It's four. I better get back. I'll miss the bus."

"Let's walk together," she tells us, and we start back down the packed dirt road through the trees.

"I've been wanting to talk to you," Mrs. Libby tells us.

We look at each other. *Yeah?*

"I think you girls have a wonderful friendship."

We don't know what to say to that.

"The thing is," she says in a careful way, "people can misinterpret closeness like yours. People might think different things."

She's warning us about something, but I still don't get it. I know Mia doesn't get it, either, by the way she's still looking expectantly at Mrs. Libby; like *okay, so?* But even as I'm thinking I don't get it, I do get it. *Lesbians.*

She's telling us that people are saying that about us. *Homos.*

It's so weird and it's so embarrassing that I almost start laughing, but Mrs. Libby is serious.

"Maybe you should start spending more time with other girls. You know, this is a wonderful school, but I've often thought that it's unnatural to pen girls up together like this. Unhealthy."

That's when I get the next part about what she's telling us—that it isn't just what other people think; she thinks so too. And I don't even know for sure what lesbians *do*.

Mia still doesn't get it. I can tell she doesn't.

"So!" Mrs. Libby says now, as we turn toward the end of the Oval, where I'll get the bus, "do you have any special plans for spring break? Will you be going home, Mia?"

"Oh, sure," Mia says. She looks at me, like *huh?*

And I try to act like I don't get it either. Because how could I talk about that with her? It would change everything. And what does it mean, anyway? Does Mrs. Libby know something about me I don't know? Aren't we just friends? Isn't anything just what it *is?*

❧

The next morning, Friday, everything's the same and nothing's the same. Tonight I'm doing acid.

On the bus out to Madeira I feel older than everybody. Eleanor, she knows nothing. The two Black girls who sit together. Nothing. The bus driver. Even Sydney Jane with her wise smile and the reddish glint in her hair, she doesn't know a thing! Not a thing! Brendan's coming by after school and we're going to drop it. That's what you say. *Drop acid.*

All day it's like a charm in my pocket and I can put my hand in there and feel it. By lunchtime I'm so wired with expectation I can't stand it. And there's something else. It's spring. It's started. The air, the promise of it.

I go into the square brick senior clubhouse. I am still thrilled by being allowed to use it. Where the big girls go. Now I'm the big girl.

There's a TV there and an old couch and a stove and everything—you can even cook if you want to. Then you step out onto the Oval like it's your yard or something. Like you have a house. The younger girls, the underclassmen, looking at you in envious awe. You act like you don't notice.

✿

After lunch I've got a free period. Some of us wind up in Mia's dorm room. I'm showing off.

"Anybody want to get high?" I say off-handedly. They can hardly believe it.

"You're crazy, Martha! You're going to get in trouble!"

"I will," says Veronica Hardsdale, who'll do anything.

"Cool," I say, and roll a joint.

Girls go in and out of the room. I tap some grass onto the yellow Zig Zag rolling paper. I'm proud of the way I can do this now. I can even talk at the same time.

"So?" I look around. "Who's coming?"

"I can't believe you're going to do that," Mia says. She almost sounds mad.

Another of the girls says, "They're going to get you someday, Martha."

I like the way that sounds; like I'm an outlaw.

I put the joint in my pocket and Veronica and I walk across campus and down into the woods near the Amphitheater. It smells like spring in the woods. The boxwoods have that wonderful spicy smell like Rosedale. The smell of the dirt. We crouch down deep in the bushes, with trees all around us and the soft far sky overhead and we smoke the joint and I feel the way it feels, the quiet hum.

"Mmmmmmm," I say to Veronica.

"Yeah," she says.

Then it's time for Creative Writing class and that's fun, too, because nobody knows and everybody knows and there's a buzz all around me like a little light. I'm the one that dares.

In Creative Writing class I feel like I've never been so creative! I'm funny and the girls laugh, and they seem dear to me now. Dear and unsuspecting with their kind, wide, Southern faces and their clean, innocent white blouses. Beside me, Mia gives me a sharp look.

"You okay?" she whispers.

I write *really stoned* on the paper in front of me and slide it toward her.

"Oh God, Martha."

Then class is over and school is over and it's the weekend finally like a badge and we all get on the bus and ride out of the gate, down through McLean and across the Chain Bridge past the cliffs and the memories and the spray-painted graffiti on the black rocks *Go St. John's* and the river and down toward Georgetown and one after another the girls get off the bus and wave good-bye, and at Wisconsin Avenue most of the rest of us get off and it's warm and I can feel how warm it is, the wonderful air of the afternoon and it's Georgetown and I am tempted to run down into the belly of it to see what's going on. But instead I have to go home and see Brendan because this is the day. And then everything after this will be after the time I took acid.

I don't know what to expect. We're in my bedroom. Brendan sits in the rocking chair and he takes two blue pills out of his pocket. They are so small.

"Are you sure?" he asks me.

"Yeah," I say.

They are so small and speckly, like teeny little bird eggs. What can they be, really?

We each take one. We don't need water. I've learned how to swallow pills without water.

"It takes a while to get off," he tells me. "About a half an hour."

He knows these things. He's gotten high before on LSD. I've only read about it. *The Electric Kool-Aid Acid Test.* Ken Kesey and the Merry Pranksters.

My room's the same. McCarthy posters and the photograph of olives and straw. The olives so shiny with oil and the colors so rich and autumnal—the green of the green, the tomatoey red of the center. The wallpaper in my room is blue and white and there are big, white billowy curtains at the windows. My bed. My desk. My stereo where I sit in the evenings listening to it turned down low. *Sweet Lorraine. Pleasures of the Harbor. Ruby Tuesday. In My Life.*

Everything's the same.

The roof outside my window and the streetlight and the trees; all the same. Things that I've been looking at all my life.

There isn't anything to talk about. We're only waiting.

Brendan sits in the chair with his long soft hair and those little wet blue eyes of his. I feel shy with him. He knows about this stuff.

"Want to go outside?" I ask him. "Want to take a walk or something?"

"Sure," he says, and we leave the house and go out and it's late afternoon already, nearly evening. Get out before my parents come home and we have to make the weary explanations.

We walk around and it's just the same at first. The brick sidewalk. The big trees reaching up. The cars parked at the curb. But then something. It's different than smoking grass. Different than the hectic rush of speed. Different than the quick jolt of poppers. Different. Something. Like I'm just starting to see things and they all look *fuller* than they usually are or something. They're wavier, like they're moving, even when they're still. The lines around the bricks in the sidewalk. The white wooden boards of the Rosedale fence.

"Let's go to the Cathedral," I tell him, and we walk that way.

I know where everything is. It's not like I'm crazy. It's just beginning.

"Are you peaking?" he asks me and I think he means peeking and I don't get why he's asking that.

He's holding my hand and his hand feels weird and spongy and big in my hand like a big soft pancake or something and I don't want to hold it but I don't want to be mean or have him know.

It's my secret.

Then there's something else; it's like I know things. What he's thinking. I could know everything if I could just concentrate on it. *I could know everything.* I could understand everything and have this sort of *power.*

I want that. I want to know everything and I already do, it turns out, but I can't say it. Because nobody else could understand the things I know. And it's so amazing—how I'm walking along thinking all these enormous things—just walking along with Brendan.

And now it's early evening—*how'd that happen?* And we're walking through the neighborhood that's just the same only it's totally different because now I can see everything!

Later we go to St. Albans where they're having some sort of coffeehouse band thing intended to keep kids off drugs. People sitting at little round tables. Some grown-up's idea of cool. The band's terrible, I guess, though it's just kids. They're young, I see. They're really young and so earnest and almost naked with their need. I can see it in the one with the guitar—the bare need in his face. And then Molly's there and Rosie and Braxton and that's cool and I smile at them and I want to tell them but then I don't want to scare them because I can see them so clearly. They might not want to be seen like that. How little Rosie is, and how fragile, with her wonderful hair like silver foil in the light. I want to touch it but you're not supposed to do that because we are not yet evolved.

I turn to Brendan and he says something, but I can't hear anything because of the loudness of the music and the lights which are also loud. You don't need lights or music because it's all just *there*. I can see odd shapes on the walls. I think they're letters. They are signs. I want to look at those for a while so I subside, but then I turn again to Brendan and he's staring forward and he looks too young and too inadequate with his hair—that hair of his—and his little eyes and I think *oh what am I doing with him?* But then he turns to me and I see he knows it too—all of it—and that we are in some way *meant*.

"Want to go?" he asks me and the idea of leaving is astounding because I feel as if I am rooted to my chair. I'm just here. And getting up seems like this enormous task and then leaving to go out into the night! But I manage and I rock against him and I feel how he feels against me and then I am embarrassed because it's like we're naked and everybody can see, but we go to the door past people who don't notice anything, who are all standing looking straight forward at the band like *that's* the whole point of the room which I guess in a way it is but it *isn't*.

"It isn't the band," I tell Brendan, and I think he gets it.

He laughs his little laugh which is light as a broom, and we go out into the black sharp night.

It's gotten colder. The Cathedral rises up like a specter with its sharp angles and its high lit sides. Like a castle. Like something medieval out of a book.

"I wish we could go down into the garden," I tell him, but instead we head across the wet black grass and back up the sidewalk toward our part of Cleveland Park. And every car that goes by has such bright, staring headlights shining much too bright! I have to put my hand in front of my face and lean against Brendan to hide from the bright glare of their eyes.

We walk around for a long time and it seems like the night is limitless and then, all of a sudden, we're back. I can see my house across the street and I know I'll have to go home and see my mother. I don't want to. I want to be back up where I was but I can tell I'm coming down, and I can't see all the twisting shapes anymore; that's over. I felt so tall and so light on my legs, but now I feel leaden in my shoes and low and exhausted and I don't remember all the stuff, just the edges, just the outlines of everything I understood. I want to go back in and claim it and drag it out with me from the attic of my own mind, the magical boxes with the prizes inside—but it's all gone.

"I have to go home," I tell Brendan and we smoke one more cigarette leaning against a parked car, both of us looking across at my house with the lights still on; somebody's waiting. It's late and I'm probably in trouble.

"Okay," I tell him. It seems too small, anything I could say, so I just say, "Okay," again and we kiss each other good night, but in a dull way, and I go across the street and up the steps of my house. 3409. The brass numbers catching the light from the street light and the dark green door.

ɕ

My dad's still up, sitting in the chair in the living room with
the newspaper across his lap. He'd fallen asleep, but he's
awake now and he looks at me.

"It's awfully late," he says and he looks old.

"I know," I tell him. I think how much I love him, how
much I want to tell him, but I only say, "I know. I'm really
sorry."

"Go to bed," he tells me.

"I'm really sorry," I say again and I mean it, but then I
think I might be overdoing it—staring at him too intensely,
so I go upstairs, but how can I sleep?

My room rushes around me.

I want to put it somewhere. Everything that's inside me.
Put it somewhere and then look at it after. I want to go to
sleep. I want to write it down. I want to go back out. Have
my exciting life.

I understand everything now.

I try to write in my journal but my hands won't work at so
fine a task.

I am in perfect controoooooolllll I write in big weird letters in
my journal. I hope that I'll remember later, what it stands
for.

I want to go to sleep but I can't sleep.

I'm supposed to work tomorrow at the Sandal Shop but
that seems so small now and so unimportant.

Everything.

I'm on the other side of some big door now, with what I
know.

What I've always known. It's what I've always wanted. It's God. That's what it is. All of this. It has to do with death and before you were born and certain books; what people write about, what people paint about, what people think about, pray about, *are* about. This is what it is. Now I know. It's like I'm in the club.

But then what? Then what do you do with it? What comes next?

🌀

I can't sleep. It's too dark and the room buzzes around me. I can't read. I'm afraid to sneak out in case I get caught. The house is too still; my parents in their bed on the other side of the wall and the buzz of the house and the room and the trees outside and I sleep at last but I wake up hot and tired.

🌀

The whole next day I drag myself through the rooms of our house. I feel sad and destroyed and uncertain. I can't go to work.

My mother comes into the living room where I am sitting in my father's chair.

"Are you okay?" she asks me.

"I don't know," I say. I don't feel angry at her this time. I feel sad. "I'm just kind of depressed."

I wish I could tell her how I'm feeling, but then I'd have to tell her about the acid. And anyway, she wouldn't understand. My mother doesn't get like this. She wouldn't let herself. She always knows what to do.

She says something kind and I remember how she can be so nice and so soft, how she used to be when we were riding in the car and I rested my face against her soft breast and my father was on one side and my mother on the other and I was there between them where I could sleep or not sleep, wake or not wake, and my sister in the backseat stretched out with her fuzzy head and we were all in the car moving forward through the night across the country going to visit our grandparents in California.

15

LIKE A CAGED THING
DENIED HER PREY

AT SCHOOL on Monday it seems like a million years since
I've been there. I don't even remember Friday afternoon,
before I tripped. I can't wait to tell Mia all about my adven-
ture. Acid. God. But it's all confused now and I don't know if
I'll be able to explain it. I'll have to take more acid to find out
how it works. All I have for a souvenir of my trip is what I
scribbled in my journal: *I am in perfect controoooooolllll.* It's not
enough.

Chapel on the floor of the gymnasium. Miss Shank in her
terrible coat. *I hate her* I whisper fiercely to Mia. She gives me
her ironic look with her light eyes, her little smile. *Yeah.*

Today Shank's talking about warning your friend when
she's in trouble. What's she even *talking* about?

Classes and more classes. The gritty glare of the March

afternoon. It's not quite spring yet, after all. Sometimes it starts to be, but then it gets cold.

Home on the bus. Everything's transformed and is the same. I feel heavy and so terrible and ancient. I'm going to have to wait forever until summer when I can finally be done with school and get out of here. Three more months.

That night I'm on the phone with Brendan in my father's study. The parents are downstairs. It's nice and quiet. I feel closer to him now after what we've been through. I might even be in love with him.

There's an emergency call; the operator interrupts us. *Emergency.* Miss Shank from Madeira.

"Martha? I need to speak to your parents. Immediately."

Later I think this must have been the way she planned it. To make it the most terrorizing of all. Or else could she have been drunk? Could she have been up in that big fancy house of hers up on the hill of the dark school campus, drinking her drinks by herself, pacing those terrible rooms, staring into her dog's eyes, furious, alone and silent?

She wasn't the one who killed the diet doctor. When I say I went to Madeira, people always say *oh wasn't that the school where the headmistress killed the diet doctor?* Yeah. But that wasn't my headmistress. That one came later. My headmistress was nuts in her own way. She was furious. Years later I found out she used to storm through the dorms at night in a rage. Rousting the girls from their beds. What did she want with them?

What does she want with me, now, on the phone?

She tells my parents that she wants us to come out to the school. I'm listening in on the other extension. *Right now.* she says. *Immediately.*

🌀

In the black backseat of our Volkswagen I ride through the darkness with my parents; the terrible, long, dark distance to Madeira. It's the same trip we take day after day on the bus, only this time there is no singing. There are no other girls. I'm stuck in the back of the bug with my parents in front, my mother twisting around in her seat to look back at me, *Do you know what this is all about?* I really don't.

I don't know which thing it is. Don't want to say it might be *this* because then again it might be *that*. Which thing is it? The skipping school? But which time? My friendship with Mia? Are we in trouble for it? It could be that. It could be anything. I could be in trouble for my grades. My outfits. My *insubordination* Miss Shank calls it. My attitude. Always with the attitude again. It could be anything. Better not guess and uncover another thing—another whole landscape that she doesn't even know about. Or does she know? She could know anything. She is enormous. What if she knows about the acid?

Or maybe it isn't me at all. Maybe it's some school-wide scandal. Maybe there's been a suicide or something. That's a good thing to think, so I'll think that. Maybe everybody is on their way out in their different cars. Maybe even Truffy Bellamy in her mother's neat gray sedan. Girls in station wagons. Suki Farber. Trish Greeley. Sydney Jane and Cassie. Everybody streaming out through the night, their mothers craning around in their front seats at them:

What's this about? Do you know what this is about?

We don't, we don't we all say.

We might know, but we're not telling.

❧

But the parking lot is empty so my dream's not true. Only two cars in the slanted spots. The quiet campus and the dead brick dorms. Two girls walking across the dark lawn with their books. It's late. I've almost never been out here at night. The library with its lights on like the interior of a refrigerator. The dark Oval in the night. Main Building with one car parked in front.

We go into the school like the doomed. My father and my mother and myself. We pass a little girl, a freshman. I don't know her name, but she knows who I am. They all know. I'm the bad one.

"What's going on?" I whisper, but she rushes off with a scared look like a rabbit. She's not part of this. She didn't do anything.

From her office we can hear Miss Shank. It's like the roaring of a foreign animal, the voice of Shank from within her cell. That office that I know, where she resides.

Some other voices, softer. Muffled sobs.

The door opens. When Veronica Hardsdale comes stumbling out with her mother and her splotchy face, I know what happened.

We go in. Of course I would have lied. But when the three of us sit there on the little couch opposite Miss Shank at her big manly desk, there is no point in lying. She knows everything.

My mother says, "Dorothy, what's this all about?"

Miss Shank ignores her, fixes me the way she does with her cold stare. Her steel eyes behind her glasses and her hard gray hair.

"Perhaps Martha can tell us." She stares right at me. "Martha, why don't you tell us what you did on Friday afternoon?"

"Veronica Hardsdale and I went down in the Amphitheater and smoked marijuana."

She's disappointed, I can tell. She wanted to roar at me. She wanted to leap out and to attack. She's like a caged thing denied her prey: the kid with the peanuts just out of reach beyond the bars. She can't yell now. I have confessed. All she can do is give a disappointed growl.

And then comes all the rest of it. We have to listen to her talk about it. How she could have me arrested. How I was endangering the school, endangering the other girls. My father serious and sober. My mother turning to look at me *where did you get it?* I make up somebody's name—a boy in our neighborhood who's always in trouble. I hardly know him. He lives on the other side of Thirty-fourth Street.

I want to be in a dream. Don't want to be here with all these grown-ups who can decide my fate. Don't want to sit in this room and hear them breathing, listen to them going on and on about it. Shank. Mother. Father. Want to leave, float out across the lawn. Go see Mia in her dorm room which I later do. They let me run across the black campus, run into her dorm and tell her like it's an emergency that I'm suspended. For three days. And then—I don't know.

✧

It's the third week in April. I'm all alone in the house. The mail comes at eleven. There might be a letter from Mia.

Sometimes she writes to me. I think of her out there, walking around where we walked, talking to other girls, sitting in Mrs. Libby's class. I wish I were there, too, but I don't know if it would be the same anymore. If we'd even still be friends. I haven't seen her in over a month, since I got expelled.

When the mailman comes I sneak downstairs and wait inside the door. He slides the mail in through the brass slot and I gently take hold of it from my side of the door. He pushes it through and I receive it, but he doesn't know I'm there.

Is he puzzled because he doesn't hear the sound of the mail hitting the floor? That slap almost like water, like an oar on waves, of magazines and envelopes flapping down onto the wooden floor? Or is he just busy and preoccupied like most people? He doesn't know I'm in here. The house, I'm sure, looks empty from the street. The blank gray windows and the quiet porch.

Today there is a letter from Antioch addressed to me. I've been waiting for it so hard that I'm afraid to even open it now that it's come. I hold it in my two hands, squeeze my eyes shut like I'm making a wish. *Please let me get in please please please.*

I take the envelope upstairs to my father's study where I'm supposed to work on my schoolwork day after day. Latin translations. Stories for Creative Writing. Algebra II.

The whole house is quiet and the rooms with all their furniture are still.

I open the letter. "We are pleased to inform you . . ."

I'm so excited! I got in! I call my mother at her office.

"Yes?" she says. That same exhaustion that she always has these days.

"I got in!" I tell her. "I got into Antioch! I can go."

"Well that's fine," she says, her voice expressionless. "Congratulations, Martha."

There's this long pause.

"I have to start this summer. Summer quarter."

"Well, that's all right," she says.

That's it? That's all she's going to say? My mother who is always so enthusiastic? Always so excited about everything whether she's furious *I'm furious with you girls!* or thrilled *I'm just thrilled!* But this pale woman—who is she? This pale voice on the phone.

"Well, you better get back to work," she tells me, and we both hang up.

🌀

Next I call Miss Shank.

"I got in!" I blurt.

"Well, Martha, you'll have to tell them that you've been expelled."

I hadn't thought of that.

"You think I ought to write them?"

"Certainly you must," she says. Her voice is faraway. I hear the hubbub of the school in the background. "And now if you'll excuse me, I have some other girls to attend to. Girls who have not been accepted into their chosen schools. Girls not as fortunate as you."

16

MY WILD FACE

IT'S REALLY HOT in Ohio. I didn't know it was going to be this hot. I'm not going to wear shoes all summer. You can go to class barefoot here. You can do anything you want. It's like a metaphor, being barefoot. Being out there, open to everything. Being stoned all the time. It's like this giant metaphor. I try to explain it to my new friend Mark. He's from Lima, Ohio and he does as much acid as I do. In fact the first night I met him he was tripping. We trip together a lot. We go into Glen Helen and take a bunch of acid and wander around and we don't even have to explain things. One of us will point at something—the way the trees are, the color of the rock, and then the other one will say *Yeah Oh Yeah I see what you mean* or something and then we both laugh. It's great. Sometimes I go to class.

It's weird being barefoot all the time metaphorically or

really. How you notice things. The black, hot asphalt outside, the cool linoleum of the floor in the dorm. Upstairs is
supposed to be girls and downstairs boys but it all gets kind
of mixed up because of how we are. We're different. The
whole campus is different. It's like this magic place outside
of time, outside of all the rest of the world: Washington,
everything, parents, where we're all from—the rest of the
world which is full of the tired old men who run the government, make wars in Vietnam, turn everything into advertising, make cruel stupid jokes, don't understand. We're
beyond all that, in this separate, stoned cool place and for the
first time in my life I feel as if I belong.

I never felt like this before. Always felt as if I didn't fit in.
As if everyone somewhere along the line had been given a set
of instructions and they'd forgotten to give them to me.

But here at Antioch I fit in. Everyone's like me.

✿

I'm barefoot. The cool linoleum in the dorm. The paths in
Glen Helen pulpy and damp. The cold cold water of the
stream. The soft bounce of the pine forest and the tall trees
where the woods looks swept.

Dancing on the stoop on a summer evening. Ed Chicken
& The French Fries playing real loud. The keg. The people
dancing and me dancing and the way I can dance. God I
could dance forever. All the music and the big wide night.

The front campus and the wide lawns and the acid night
and somebody's dorm room with the windows open to the air
that's still and dark.

The bathroom.

I'm tripping. I come in late and there's someone in the shower and I don't know if it's more than one person. Is there a boy in our bathroom and will I have to see him naked? My face in the mirror over the sinks. How it looks. My eyes look wild. The pupils are so big—I'm afraid of how big they are—will they take over my eyes entirely? Will I go blind? The room is bright too bright. My face looks blotchy and red in the mirror and I have this big weird grin on my face. I'm famous for my grin but it's sort of scary and unreal late at night in the mirror the sight of my enormous grin the teeth the big red gums my wild eyes. My hair sticks out all over. The skin of my face is red and I can see every pore and these weird lines on my face and I think of my grandmother saying, "I look in the mirror and I don't know who that is, that old woman. I don't know my face."

I don't know my face and I want to put cold water on it something that will wash it clear of this mad expression. Noise in the shower behind me. Somebody might come in. It's two A.M.

I can't sleep. I don't ever sleep anymore. Don't want to sleep in the night which is the time when the dances are, when the campus is wild.

Somebody said there's a party in South Hall on the other side of campus. It's condemned but people live there and some of the art students have studios there. There's a bat nailed to the door. A real one, dead. Can I go by myself?

Somebody will go with me. A bunch of us. I like it when there's a bunch of us. Boys from the rooms downstairs. Mark. Maybe the boy with the black hair who doesn't do acid. But then he does do it and a year or so later I hear that he might have killed himself. *You're kidding me. Yeah I know, but I think it was him.*

We all go out across the campus. *Be quiet!* somebody yells from their dorm room. Somebody who doesn't get it—how the campus is, how it's meant to be—the summer campus of Antioch. It's not for studying. Not for carrying your books under your arm for gods sake as if you were back in high school. Not for sitting in classes and raising your hand and doing your homework at your goddam desk! This is Antioch! This is Yellow Springs! Aren't we enlightened past that?

There are factions of course. There are real students here, but I don't know any of them. Maybe that one boy, the one with the glasses who wants to be a scientist or something. Can't figure out how he got in our dorm. And my roommate who turns out to be pretty straight. *Has smoked pot* she tells me *a couple of times* but takes herself seriously and *would never do anything* she tells me *to mess up her mind.* Oh my god she doesn't get it at all.

I'm the one who gets it.

Come on! I shout at the rest of them.

Oh man. someone says. *Oh man Martha!* I love how that sounds—like I'm completely crazy. We take off.

I still don't have any shoes on. I love that I don't have shoes on and it's three or something three in the morning and we're all sneaking out of the dorm but you don't have to sneak because nobody cares but the tired voice from one of the rooms yells out again, *Will you be quiet out there? Some of us want to sleep!* and we put our hands up over our mouths and giggle because it's so funny and make these big faces like *oh yeah Mr. So and So* and then out and across the dark lawns there's a path, isn't there a path?

The campus at night is so magic. It feels completely safe though of course it isn't. It used to be. Some of the bearded, older fifth-year students tell us how it used to be. *You never locked your dorm* etc. etc. *you just left your wallet.* Yeah yeah yeah. But this is the Antioch we know. You lock your dorm and somebody got raped but we don't care. It won't happen to us because we're in a pack.

That's the thing about it. We're in a pack all the time. We're like a pack of furry animals. Funny animals.

I want to try this out on Mark. *They can't tell,* I tell him, grabbing his arm. His arm feels flimsy underneath his baggy denim jacket. Flimsy. He's so tall.

They can't tell if we're young or old. They can't tell if we're male or female.

And then he doesn't do anything stupid like ask me *who can't?* Because right away he gets it.

Yeah, he says. *They don't know. They can't even tell us apart!*

We're walking really big now; our long strides. Across the campus past the still hull of the Student Union silent in the night, the Inn where parents stay when they come to visit. The brick buildings, dorms, and then the long stretch of grass and there South Hall and there the dark dim lanterns

lie. It looks a little scary, like something out of a fairy tale—
dark tall building against the dark night sky.

✿

I want to call out to that girl, to that old self of mine as she
rushes across the night campus. *Where do you think you're
going?* No, not that. That would sound too much like my
mother. I want to call out to her, *Wait, come back here. Come
here a minute! Let me talk to you.*

But she's not stopping to talk to anyone, certainly not to
me, this grown-up person I've become. This bank director,
this professional fundraiser, this grandmother who gets up
every morning four A.M. to work at her computer. That girl
didn't even know what a computer was.

She won't stop. She doesn't recognize me. This tall narrow
pinched-up woman I've become. In bed by eight-thirty.
Doing the daily crossword from the *Bangor Daily News*. Getting my dutiful exercise at the gym. Grown up. Divorced
and prosperous and with my shiny car and careful house. My
dishwasher. My garbage disposal. My neatly lined up shelves
of books. My dowdy Lands End cotton sweater and my Dan-
sko clogs.

What would she do—that girl—if I approached her on
the dark campus? Ran after her? I can still run fast. I can
probably run faster now than she—with her cigarettes and
her bare feet and her floppity breasts under her Indian bedspread dress, her wads of shabby, sweaty hair. Her wild
face.

What would she do if I ran after her and grabbed her arm and said, *Hey, wait, look at me! Look at me! I'm you!*

You're not me! I don't know you!

Yes! I am! I tell her. I stare right into her face. *I am you. I'm you in thirty years. I'm you grown up and disappointed by the disappointments of life. I'm you after all the drugs and the adventures. I'm you after all the craziness is past. I'm you with what you've left me.*

I don't want to be you. She looks at me with her crazy eyes. *I don't want to be you with all your disappointments! I don't want to be you dyeing your hair to hide the gray. I don't want gray! I don't want your wrinkles and your back that hurts and the surgery scar on your belly. I don't want your house and your car and your paid-off mortgage and your grown-up children and your grown-up boyfriend and your grandchild and your bank account and your dull straight boring life in Maine.*

That isn't how I want to live. That isn't how I want to end up.

I'm mad at her. I'm furious with her. *What do you mean? You're lucky I've got even this to show you, after what you did to me. Wrinkles? Of course I've got wrinkles. You laid me out in the sun for hours and hours to wrinkle me up like this. You're lucky I'm still alive with all you did to me—you and your hundred hits of acid. You and your many sexual partners. You and your freedom and your bare feet. Lucky you didn't cut your feet on something, kill yourself with all your reckless ways. Get some incurable disease. Go nuts. Fall out a window. Get busted and get put away for twenty years. Get raped and murdered hitchhiking around the country. Get lost. You could have gotten lost. You tried so hard to come unhinged from everything. You said it was for freedom, peace, some cockamamie combination of psychedelia and Sixties radicalism and a mish-mash poetic religious philosophy you patched together from Kerouac and Kesey and bits of conversation that you overheard.*

✺

Come on, the other kids (they're all kids!) call to her. *Come on, Martha!*

They can't see me.

And she can't see me, really see me. Only the dark shape of my desperation. A lonely car goes by. Someone patrolling the campus late at night. The light slides by us, covers our faces like a cloth for a moment, like a white cloth.

If I could pull her away from all of this. If I could stop her now before the rest of it. I know what comes next—the parts that I remember—the crazy nights, the bad apartment in the Haight, the hitchhiking, the jail cell, the drugs, the drugs, the boys, the men. I know what comes. I know how fast she spins. And I know what comes after and the slow, sad, endless rehabilitation she'll have to go through. And the shame from it that she'll refer to with bravado for a few years, and then she'll just ignore.

I know what comes.

But I can't reach her. I can't touch her. I am fading from this scene. I'm losing her.

I see her toss her head like a wild horse in the campus night. She has to get to the party and I have to get back to reality, which I have chosen over all of that.

❀

"What were you doing back there?" Mark asks me. "I thought we were going to South Hall."

I shake my head, grab him by the hand. "Come on!" I yell, and we charge forth into the night.

❀

It's a hot, still day, mid-August. A bunch of us have come to the quarry to go swimming. Sometimes we come here at night to go skinny-dipping, but now on an August afternoon the quarry's full of families and little children lying on their bellies in the shallow water letting it lap at them. I haven't had much sleep. Been up all night tripping on mescaline. Still sort of feel it in me. Mark's here and Dexter; Tucker and Deb. Zap from the town, and Sally. We came in someone's truck, a bunch of us in back like migrant workers with our ripped-up cutoffs and our dirty feet.

The families of Ohio got here first. They're making a day of it; the young fathers with their sunburnt shoulders and their crew-cut hair. The women who aren't really much older than we are, but married and with all their little children. Sand pails and the piles of rocks they found. Their picnics and the sound of radio music and the hot, still air.

We find a place along the shore.

"It's so big in the day," somebody says.

"Yeah," Tucker says, who's from here, "be careful. It's real nice to swim here, but there're deep spots. You feel it getting cold, that means it goes way down. You got to watch yourself."

The mothers watching their children through their sunglasses. The lazy sound of bugs and birds. The sky.

I lie on a blanket from my dorm. I feel like a kid again, lying on a beach somewhere my mother nearby and the quiet day.

"You okay?" Tucker asks me. "You up all night again, you naughty thing?"

"Yeah, most of it."

I'm so tired. Drifting through the last drifts of the trip. The shreds of mescaline like petals and the slow meandering back. Like ambling down some quiet road. "The petals . . ." I say slowly.

"Yeah."

Tucker likes us fine but he's practical. From town and from the country. Has his truck, is making something of his life. Taking some courses. Painting houses. Working at the Inn.

"You kids," he'll say and shake his head from side to side like an old man, sadly. "You kids are ruining your lives." But we think he's just joking.

Last night men walked on the moon. We all went over to Tucker's place to see it. The grainy guys on TV with their cardboard-looking flag that snapped out flat after they stuck it in the ground. The arrogance of claiming the moon! Their little voices.

"We're seeing history," somebody said and then we all laughed, stoned.

I went out into the night outside. The shabby, quiet summertime Ohio road. The little bunched-together houses of Yellow Springs, the quiet neighborhood where Tucker lived.

So different from the clash and swirl of campus. I'd live out here, I thought. Someday out here.

Mark came out too. He'd taken the same stuff I took, but not as much.

We wandered out into the road a little ways; down past the quiet houses. We looked up, and Mark put his arm around my shoulder. We were pals.

"You see it up there?" he asked. "You see the moon?"

I stared up hard into the far, lost sky. I saw it big and bigger in the night. The moon enormous bright gigantic and I was sure that I could see them there, like ants. "I see them!" I told Mark. "The men up there! I see them."

"Yeah," he said. "I think I see them too."

I think about these lost things now in the sleepy stunned sun of the day lying by the water at the quarry. The sound of the children playing all around me. Tucker there and the boys from town. Deb in her old green bathing suit. And Sally from Peoria in her bikini. We're all lying around on top of one another. My head on Mark's leg. Sally's hair flopped over my arm. I was right. We are a tribe.

Drifting in and out of consciousness. Drifting with the sound of the afternoon. Somebody's radio, the songs I love. Everything so beautiful and sweet.

"You want to go into the water? You're getting red," Tuck asks me.

"Yeah, okay," I say, and slide or sort of roll myself the last few feet into the water that feels like ribbons so light on my skin.

Here near the shore it's shallow. You can lie there and just let it lap over your hot skin, and the feel of it so lovely. Sally smiles at me a sleepy smile. Her face is too red, too. We're all getting sunburned but it doesn't matter.

"This is like heaven," I say.

Tucker: "Well, yeah. This is a nice place. And this is the best day we're going to have all summer. This is the last good time we'll have here at the quarry."

I roll around and swim away from shore. I can hear the radio and the children but go farther. It's bigger than it looks from shore. The wide sky overhead, the trees. The water comes up around the sides of my face as I lie on my back and float there.

Drifting. Drifting. And then I turn again and swim farther out and I can feel it—what Tucker told us—the cold part underneath. Look down and can't see anything, no bottom, nothing; just the dark, still depths, the cold, dark water that goes down and down.

I lift my head back up and gasp for air. I don't want to look into that scary dark space—want to be out here in the sky. The warm top water and the kids and mothers and the day.

I don't want to look back down in there.

I kick and twist in the water and swim back toward the shore where all the people are, and pull myself up onto the sandy bank again.

"You okay, Martha?" Tucker asks.

"Yeah," I say. "I didn't like the cold part out there."

"That's where it's deep," he says.

We stay there all afternoon lying on the blanket, talking once in a while. I guess I doze. Then it's time to pack up the stuff and get back. Tucker has to work at the Inn that night and I'm so tired. We all got too much sun. Some of the other little families are leaving, and some teenagers have come and are playing their radios now, but louder and obnoxious. "Yeah, let's go."

We walk the rim of the quarry, back to where the truck is parked. Pass a bunch of town boys with their hairy legs and cutoffs and a cruel look.

One of them yells something at us, but I can't understand it. Something about *dirty hippies* probably or *dope smoking* or *fags,* but I can't tell.

Zap's big and all he has to do is show that he's with us and they shut right up. They know him anyway. He's from the town.

We climb up into the truck and we're just getting ready, waiting for Sally, when we hear the yelling.

"Help! Help! He's drowning!" in a gurgly voice.

Is that one drowning? Which one? The one that's yelling?

"Help! He's down there! He's drowning!"

I freeze in the back of the truck but the boys run back—Zap and Tucker and even Mark who looks inconsequential, floppy, loping past. And Dexter runs back, too.

They all run back but I just sit there on the old tire in the back of the truck hearing that terrible voice.

"Oh God help!"

Then all the yelling and the hurry and confusion. I can't

go back there. Deb coming up to the truck from the other side, "What happened?"

"I don't know," I say.

I hear another terrible scream.

I feel like wood.

✧

Later on Tucker comes to my dorm room. "I thought you'd want to know. That kid this afternoon? They got him to the hospital. He's in a coma."

And a few days after that we heard that he was dead.

17

BOWLING IN OHIO

I BUY 100 HITS of acid at the beginning of winter quarter for $100. They're pink. If I sell 50 at $2 each, I'll have my money back, and then I can take all the rest.

I have to wait a day between trips or I won't get off—but then it turns out if I take two, or maybe three, I can still get high.

❧

It's night. It's so cold in the winter in Ohio. I don't feel like taking acid. I feel like taking something different. Somebody has some caps of something. They said that it's organic. Brown powdery stuff in a big clear cap. It looks too big to take. Too large to swallow, and too brown. What is it? Some kind of horse tranquilizer? Somebody said that, but maybe they were kidding. Some kind of hallucinogenic shit. I think it's like peyote, so that's cool. But will it make me throw up? I don't want to throw up. I don't like that feeling.

I remember lying in my bed, eight or nine years old, in my bed in Washington at night. Lying in bed after some big weird familial Thanksgiving dinner at the Truesdales'. Lying in bed and seeing again and again the terrible half-hacked carcass of the turkey. Not wanting to see it but shutting my eyes and seeing it. The gaping cavity. The piles of grayish stuffing. The big full plates. Not wanting to see but seeing the seas of thick brown gravy. The piles of potato and the glasses full of water that didn't taste like our water at home. The ice was different. Made in different shapes. Mechanical shapes; too flat, too narrow. Not like our honest big square cubes my mother made in the old-fashioned metal ice trays. These ice cubes were made in a machine that roared and rattled in the kitchen all through dinner. We could hear it. What was that? *It was the ice machine,* somebody said.

And now, hot, lying in my bed, staring upward, it was all I could see—the sight of those terrible, alien ice cubes. The taste of that alien water. The sight of the hacked-at carcass of the bird. And I was going to. I didn't want to. I was going to throw up. I didn't want to, I was going to. I was going to! A big lumpy stream would come choking, coughing out of me. I would throw up and throw up and throw up.

Will it make me throw up? I don't want to.

No.

And then we were high again and racing across the campus. It was cold but it didn't matter. We'd go down into the Glen. We'd go downtown through the strange, old-fashioned Ohioan streets of Yellow Springs. The houses and the people, all unconscious and beautiful in their unconsciousness. The bare trees and the sullen snow.

We were high and there was a dance in the Caf with Clean Gene and his Record Machine. James Brown. Otis Redding. Lee Dorsey: *Everything I do gon' be funky, from now on.* The Temptations.

Roaring back into the dorm in the middle of the afternoon. I was out all night. I don't know where I was. The girl in the hallway, Debbie Something, with her plain dull face, catches my arm.

"Martha?"

I stare at her. I have big eyes.

"Martha, are you okay?"

I stare at her, grinning my wildest grin.

"I'm fine!' I laugh at her worry. *She reminds me of something. What.*

"Martha, we're worried about you."

"Worried?" I laugh at her and my laugh sounds ragged.

Who does she reminds me of? Someone.

"Martha, I think you're doing too many drugs. Maybe you ought to slow down."

Slow down? And then what? And then what would I be?

I give her my wild, careless laugh. I say, "I'm okay. I'm fine."

I shake off her hand and run away. She reminds me of someone from way back, a long time ago.

I want this. This is what I want. This is how you experience Life.

But then the dull parts in between. I feel sad and leaden, ordinary, stunned with the world. Walking across campus feels like walking on the outside of the swimming pool after you've been swimming all afternoon—after you've been weightless and now, soggy in your saggy suit, you're big and dull and stumpy, barefoot, short.

I don't want that. I don't like that part.

🌀

I wake up and my mouth tastes terrible, and the room smells funny and there's junk all over and the dull light blares in from the windows and there's somebody in the bed beside me that I hardly know. Somebody whose face is not as I imagined it last night stoned at the dance—not elfin, magical, and not angelic, but puffy, pasty, with some weird kind of scraggly too-young beard and zits and greasy hair already (and he's only twenty) thinning. And I don't know him. I don't recognize his skin. I don't like the smell of him now this morning waking up in the bed. I want to run away. Get up out of the bed, pull something on to hide myself, and run away. I want to go and shower shower shower. Get away. But this is my room and I have to wait, instead, for him to go.

But then if he goes, then what? Then who am I? Then I would want him back. Because anything. Even him. Even this dull boy with his zits and his greasy thinning hair hanging down in some terrible approximation of a rock star but a skinny, nerdy, pale-skinned rock star with too many pores— even he is better than the loneliness, than the sudden terror that overtakes me. And I hate him. And I hate myself. And I hate when he gets up out of the bed and I see even more of his skin and I see him pull on his stupid white underpants which remind me of my own father's underpants and fit him oddly, make him look wide, wrong-shaped, sloppy, and I see his terrible testicles in there all droopy and his penis slung off to the side, soft and lolling like an unhealthy worm, and I see the zits on his back and I hope I didn't catch them, catch anything from him. Catch crabs. Catch gonorrhea. But I doubt I did. After all, we're all at Antioch College. We're all from the same kind of homes, aren't we? We're all kind of rich.

That's when I think I hate him most of all—in his underpants. But then I hate him even more when he pulls on his jeans and I see he's done that nerdy thing people do—cut up the seam of their pants and sew in a triangle of some cloth— paisley or something—to turn their regular jeans into bell-bottoms. Only it doesn't work because the cloth is too floppy and thin and the jeans sort of close up over it and it's not cool and it doesn't look good and I want to tell him *It doesn't look good it's not cool* but then he might look at me the way people get to look at you—like *you're* the one who doesn't get it, and he might say something like—*why does it have to be cool?* Like it's *your* hang-up and he's probably right, it probably *is* my hang-up and I hate him for knowing that about me—that I care. That's when I really hate him—when he puts on his shirt and bumbles around for his shoes under the bed and he's got cowboy boots or something *natch* I hear myself saying internally *natch* like my sister would say making fun of him and I miss my sister and I miss everybody I know, my sister, my friends—my real friends from high school, from when I was a kid. I miss my parents. Even my parents. Even my mother. Especially my mother, because suddenly I am in this room that's supposed to be my room with this person I had sex with and none of it feels real, and none of it has anything to do with my life.

I better get high.

You want to get high? I ask him. Because here he is and maybe if we were high I could get it back—some of the feeling I had last night. We must have had some—some kind of connection; he must have seemed real to me.

But he shakes his head.

I'm too weird for him.

We could go over to the Glen, smoke a joint or something I say and I hate how I sound. Wheedly and desperate, and he shakes his head; *no, he has stuff he has to do.*

And so I lie back on the bed and shut my eyes like I don't care; wait for him to leave because the room smells weird and I hope it's not me. It's him that smells like that. So he's used to it. I want him to go if he's not going to stay and fall in love with me and be my boyfriend. Because I have to pee but I don't want to get up and stand there naked in front of him, now that he's dressed.

❧

I am marching across the campus in the snow. I'm too high. It's so cold out. If I walk and I walk really fast I won't be quite as high. Last week Dexter and I hitchhiked to his uncle's house in West Virginia. We took acid a couple of times when we were there. It was really good stuff and we walked like this up and down the streets of the town so we wouldn't be so high. Later Dexter sat in a big chair with his earphones on listening to *Here Comes the Sun* with this weird expression on his face like he was dead.

I don't know what I'm supposed to be doing. I just walk along on the crusty white snow, just walk across the campus toward South Hall. I know some people in there. Maybe I'll get high with Howard. I already am high. *Oh, yeah.*

❧

I'm taking Bowling for my Phys Ed credits. We go on Friday evenings to a bowling alley on the way to Xenia. We carpool, but I don't have a car. I thought it would be kind of fun—a little funky: bowling in Ohio. But it turns out that this class is serious. Everyone in the class but me is Black. Even the teacher—Black. But not the Black ones from the Angry Black Dorm, the ones who have their own private dances on the back stoop outside the C Shop, the ones who stare out of their Black dorm with their angry faces, talk only to one another, have their Afros, no. These are the straight ones. Girls with processed hair and little dresses. They actually get dressed up for Bowling! They're nice. They're very nice, but it's like we're separate animals. Like they go to some other Antioch—some regular college where there are regular classes and sororities or something. They don't get it, I think, but I do.

I like to take some acid right before the class. I figure if I can get through bowling, then I'll get off right in time for the Friday night dance. But it doesn't always work right, and sometimes it hits too soon, and then it's a little bizarre to be in the bowling alley getting higher and higher with all those girls with their processed, shiny black hair in a flip and their skirts and their bowling lingo which I never learned, never having been a bowler before, and none of them know what's going on with me—the girl in the Indian bedspread dress and the cowboy boots and the wild, wild hair. None of them know. They just think I'm weird, or a terrible bowler. When I stand there at the shiny wooden runway where I know the ball is supposed to go, stare down toward the far pins, I feel this rush of ecstasy and understanding and I turn to smile at them but they are talking among themselves and do not see me.

They are hunching over the indecipherable score card which I don't understand, but luckily I hardly ever knock anything down, so I don't have to.

Whoosh! comes the sound all around me, the clanking of pins like bottles, the knocking around of the metal arm that comes down and shoves them over. It's like. It's like . . . if Mark were here I could explain it. If Dexter were here. But they're not, so I just hurl the bowling ball haphazardly and it slides over inevitably into the alley and runs down inside, making its lost, clanking descent, and one of the girls says,

"Nice try, Martha!" They all know me. I'm the White One.

I decide it's better not to say anything in the car. It's so cold out. We all leave the bowling alley and pack back into the car and I don't say a word, though my breathing sounds kind of loud to me. I hope I'm not roaring. Or is that just how we all breathe all the time? Maybe it just sounds loud because I'm tripping.

It's such a relief to be back on the campus. I get out of the car and I wave in a glad way like everything's normal and go off to the dance at the Caf.

It's so cold that the windows get steamed up and cloudy. Clean Gene Lohman is playing *Pop Corn* by James Brown, and *Sex Machine. Get on up!* Pete's dancing the way he dances, with little half-interested steps, holding his hands flapped down like droopy paws. He's very cool. He's dancing with the girl he's seeing now who has a blank expression, and she dances just like him. There's the boy with the curly hair Chris Something who is manic on the dance floor. He goes so fast and jittery that nobody can keep up. And Fargo, with his long hair and his floppy expression and the girl who's still a virgin does that sweepy thing with her arms that irritates me. But mostly I just dance. I can dance and dance and dance. I keep on dancing. Sometimes it's cool and tight and controlled the way Black people dance. Sometimes I'm a hippie and loose like Fargo and do this stuff with my shoulders. Sometimes there's a lot of foot stuff going on. I love it all.

"You sure can dance," somebody says to me, some guy who's standing there. I'm sweaty. I think he might be a professor. He's kind of cute, but he's old. I feel triumphant and

unafraid. By the end of the night I will be entirely dancing.
Hair flopping with thick sweat. Wearing my short blue
Indian cotton dress and my cowboy boots all sharp and defi-
nite, my rings, my hair.

I feel good. I'm high but I don't feel too high. I'm surrounded by people and we're all communicating in some way
by dancing. You can dance right up to somebody and sort of
hook into their dance and then dance away. So we're all sort
of communicating with one another with the dancing, with
the music—all of us—but no one has to talk.

Outside hot steam rushes out into the cold night. My hair
freezes on the way back to the dorm. I could do anything.
Could run across the campus if I wanted. Who's awake? Who
wants to come with me?

✿

But then sometimes. Sometimes in between dances, or when
I'm coming down, or when nobody's around in the dorm.
Where are they? Classes? Then sometimes I feel this sad
ache. This loneliness. I have to do something. Eat something.
Read something. Go somewhere. I can't be with myself.

✿

It's the end of winter quarter. Everybody's leaving. And it's
still not spring. It's cold and gray day after day on the Antioch campus. There's a big dance at the end of the quarter—
Div Dance. The extravaganza. The endless Saturday night. It
starts out with a variety show in Kelly Hall.

The band gets up on stage. Ed Chicken & the French Fries. Kiki Williams, tall as a statue, long and skinny with her long black hair. Her boyfriend Tag who's handsome and mean-looking with a scar on his lip and his long black hair too, and his dirty pants. The drummer is like all drummers—hesitant and weird and speedy with frizzy gingery hair and glasses and a bowed, almost concave body and a Southern accent. Then Danny Greene, the one I secretly have a crush on. He's from Tulsa, Oklahoma and he's quiet and he plays guitar, and when he plays—even though I don't understand what they're singing, and I don't even like the kind of music that they play—I like him. I like his gypsy face. His curly black hair. His beautiful dark eyes. I've seen him in the Caf, walking across the campus in his beat-up leather jacket and his derby hat.

They play and people are getting up out of their chairs and dancing in the aisles of Kelly Hall and waving their arms and Kiki is yowling into the mic, and it's so loud and it's so late and the acid is coming on stronger and stronger and I have to get out of here, have to push past people dancing in their places, have to shove my way and I say *Sorry,* and *Excuse me* but I can't hear my own voice as I push my way out of the auditorium into the hall, down the stairs, out into the cold black night where suddenly everything is quiet and dark and I can hear one person howl like a wolf from somewhere far across the campus and then, there they are—the wholesome folk dancers dancing together, students and professors fat and in twirling skirts and they are doing their folk dance here on the snowy brick square on the last night of the quarter and they don't even seem to see me as I walk by.

✿

The campus is almost emptied out. The dorms are silent.
One bicycle lies on its side on the brown lawn.

"Hey," Danny Greene says, and comes over to sit beside
me in the Caf. "We're the only ones left. You look like a
friend of mine. A girl who got killed."

So then we begin our romance on the empty campus, in
the chilly room of the empty Dawson Dorm. The beds have
already been stripped. The posters are off the walls. Rosa's
black light, gone. The cleaning lady says that I can stay there
a few more days if I don't mess it up.

He lives in an apartment off-campus with Tag and Kiki.
One whole room is wallpapered with egg cartons "for sound"
he tells me.

✿

We're in his room. It's night. The rest of them are all upstairs
or something. Danny's sitting on the backseat of a car that he
has for a couch in his room. He's got his guitar.

"You want a hear a song I wrote?"

I do.

He fiddles with the guitar, plays a few chords. He looks
different playing here in the room than he does when he's on
stage. It's private, how his face looks, like he's alone. I feel
privileged to be here.

Then he starts playing and I can tell that this is where it is
that he's most real.

"My chevvy needs a rain job," he sings. *"My momma said don't smoke dope it ain't good for you."*

His fingers are clever on the strings of his guitar, holding them down here, here and here; while he strums with his right thumb, while he hunches forward over his guitar and sings and looks at me.

"And in this furrow we'll plant corn and in this furrow we'll plant peas but in your furrow, is where I want to be-ee."

He holds his mouth a certain way when he is singing and when he looks at me his face looks like the face he has when we're in bed together. But this, in a way, is more intimate: him singing to me this song that he made up.

🌀

Later, we're lying on the mattress in his room, and he pulls the sleeping bag up over us and it's like we're in this secret little cave together.

"What do you think about, when you're writing songs?" I ask him.

He tightens his arms around me and I feel held in a way that I have never been held since I was a child.

"I don't know," he says. "I'm thinking about the song. I'm in the music. I guess it's the one time I don't have to think."

"I know just what you mean," I say.

I do.

🌀

He seems old to me and certain of himself. He has a car, a blue VW. He drives it around campus dodging the winter potholes. When he looks at me he has an expression that I love to see. This time I don't even have to wonder what it is. We are in love.

🌀

Danny's going to Europe. He's going to travel around, he tells me, just see stuff. Next fall he's going to Switzerland to study with Piaget. He's going to be a psychologist. It's the most grown-up thing I can imagine.

He treats me the way none of the boys has ever treated me. Like I am precious. And he has a beard. He's Jewish. When we talk about God and acid he knows what I mean. He knows what I'm talking about. Everything seems like a sign.

And I remind him so much, he tells me, of his friend that died in a motorcycle accident a year ago. They were best friends. They used to bake bread together. They talked and talked. One time they did make love but it was just like baking bread he tells me. When she had the motorcycle crash they were in California, and he heard about it and he started rushing out to where it was, but then he stopped, he said, because he realized he didn't want to see her body. This is his story. His story is about growing up in Tulsa. Playing music. Riding in trains to visit his relatives in Chicago.

My stories are precious to him, too. Rosedale. Madeira. Getting kicked out. The McCarthy campaign. The apartment in San Francisco. Brendan. Poetry. My father's journeys and my mother's face.

"Your parents sound really nice," he tells me. "It sounds as if they really love you."

"Yeah," I say. "I guess they do."

18

MY FATHER

BUT WHEN I get back to Washington it's springtime and the house is empty. My mother's at the office. My sister's studying in Paris. My dad's in Vietnam covering the war that's never going to end. We've invaded Cambodia now.

I'd sort of forgotten about the war when I was in Ohio, San Francisco. It was like war and politics had nothing to do with my life. But now that I'm home again, it's my oblivion that seems unreal.

It's like I've been in a big noisy matinee and now I totter out into the flat plain brittle daylight.

❦

I'm alone in the house. The phone rings and it's Brendan, my old boyfriend.

"You want to get together?"

"Sure," I say, but I'm not sure at all.

"I'm only here for about four days," I tell him. "I'm going to Europe with this guy I met."

I like the way that sounds.

"We've got a van."

His voice is light, the way that I remember it. "Oh yeah?" he says. "I'll meet you up at Rosedale."

So I walk up there, through the abundance that is Washington in spring. Up Newark Street, the herringbone brick sidewalk. The trees overhead, their filled-up branches, flowery with leaves, almost meeting over the quiet street. Cars at the curb. The houses with their porches. It's all the same.

He's waiting for me where we used to go, deep in the boxwoods. I've got a short dress on, so when I sit down I can feel the cool, damp earth against my thighs. He's already smoking a joint and hands it over. He doesn't look any different; this whole year later.

"Hi," he says, like we used to say. The few times we lay together when our parents were away, on secret afternoons up in my bedroom, stoned and shy with one another, we would turn, and our faces would be so close and *hi,* we'd say. And it meant all these other things, at least I thought so. But now, when he says it, he just sounds young. He's still in high school. I can't believe it.

I take the joint so I don't have to look at him. It's shadowy in here inside the boxwoods.

"So you're going to Europe?"

"Yeah," I tell him. "There's this guy."

"I know, you told me." He sounds sullen.

"Well, what did you think? I've been away a year," I tell him. "All this stuff has happened."

"Yeah."

"It's been wild," I tell him. "Antioch is pretty cool. And I was out in San Francisco for my co-op."

"Yeah," he says.

I want him to know all this stuff I've done. Acid probably a hundred times. All the visions I've had, all the big things I've figured out. Golden Gate Park that one day in October. Hitchhiking to Chicago. Yosemite and the Berkeley Hills. He's just been here.

"I can't believe I only started tripping last year," I tell him.

"Yeah, well you know what? I've been doing stuff too," he says, as if he's heard me, everything I've been thinking, sitting there in the dirt. "You're not the only one who's had this year."

I stare at him. He's never talked like this to me before.

"Huh?"

"You're not the only one," he says again.

And then I think he's going to get up and storm out of there or something. I'm a little stoned now, so I can almost imagine how the hard, tiny leaves of the boxwoods would shake and quiver as he brushed through the branches. He's that mad.

But he doesn't. He just says that, and then he's quiet and he puts the joint out in the dirt and lights a cigarette.

"I gotta go," he tells me.

"My dad's been sick," he says.

✿

We're bombing in Cambodia. There's going to be a huge demonstration down at the Reflecting Pool. I want to go, but Mother says it's too dangerous in the same voice she used to say *Don't open the door, girls. Don't tell them I'm not home.*

She goes to New York for two days on business. Before she leaves, she tells me again not to go to the demonstration, as if she can stop me. She doesn't know anything about me—all I've done. It's a National Day of Protest! I'm embarassed at how I've been on vacation from reality. I know all this stuff now—all this stuff about Love and Peace and God and all the rest. About the Universe. How it all fits together. I should be *using* it. Using it to make the world better. Or something.

I haven't been to a protest in years. At Antioch the radicals were a separate group—black haired with thick black mustaches, dark sideburns, burly shoulders. They were serious and sat together in the Caf. There were different sects—the Black militants, the feminists, and the male radicals who were sort of rude and mean to women and regarded the rest of us—the floppier, hairier, dancing hippies—as a bunch of useless jerks.

I want to be part of that again—to feel that rush of indignation—that almost mentholated, cleansing, self-congratulatory sense of righteousness and rage. A sense of purpose.

✿

But then that morning in our still house the phone rings and I think it might be Cassie or Sydney Jane or somebody—

some old friend—but it's my mother calling from New York. Is she checking up on me again? Like she used to after I got kicked out of Madeira? But her voice sounds different now.

I look out of the back window of my father's study where at night for years I've heard him typing and typing on his old black Royal typewriter. It is the sound of my childhood. When I heard him typing I knew that everything would be all right.

The backyard is sweet and green and full of flowers and on the phone my mother says, "Daddy's been captured. He's near Phnom Penh. We don't know where he is."

What? I ask her. *What?* Because my father goes to Vietnam all the time and he's careful. He always tells us how careful he is. *There are the hawks and there are the doves* he says *but I'm a chicken.* And he doesn't go in the opium dens with the other reporters. And he doesn't go where they're bombing or catch rides on scary airplanes. He's careful. And he was careful, even this time, we hear later. He and two other reporters in a jeep heading into Cambodia, stopped at a checkpoint, taken.

❧

And then nothing matters at all and I go downtown anyway with some of the Moores and the crowds are big and it's hot and sunny and it feels more like a be-in or a celebration than a protest. People with their faces painted and weird clothes and everybody loving everybody else and handing things to one another—beads, food, lemonade, joints, flowers, cigarettes. We all love everything. My father's gone.

❧

That night there's a sort of vigil at our house. They don't know where he is. My mother's still in New York. She calls me up and doesn't ask me where I've been. People keep turning up. Doris Perleman from the McCarthy campaign. Becca Moore and Leo from across the street. Cassie and Sydney Jane. We all sit around in my parents' living room and it feels like we're the grown-ups. I sit in my father's chair, and we talk about my father. There's no news. They think he's still alive.

I'm sure he'll be all right, my mother said over the phone in this new voice she's got.

We smoke some pot and talk about my father. Everybody loves him. I didn't realize. I thought I was the only one who knew him.

"You know, in the campaign," Doris tells us, "I got to know a lot of the reporters. And they were really terrible, some of them. You'd get to know them and they'd act like they wanted to talk to you but sooner or later they'd always hit on you, but not Richard Dudman, not your father. Always a gentleman."

And then I think of my father in a new way, as a man, not just my father. And everything about him seems dear to me. My dad when we were little, walking down Newark Street with us on summer afternoons after work. Sitting on the side of the swimming pool, letting us ride on his feet. I always knew how much he loved us. When he was reading to us. When he listened to me when I told him things, even terrible things, I always knew how much he loved me. That never wavered. Not when I was little, not later when I was dirty and lost, not when I came home late, not when I got bad grades, got kicked out of school, I always knew that to my father I was precious.

I can't imagine being in a world where he's not there.

❧

My mother and I go shopping at Lord & Taylor in Bethesda. My father's still missing but I'm going to Europe anyway, my mother tells me. *We don't know how long it's going to be.* They've got people working on it—working on getting him out. The newspaper's working on it. People in the government. Prince Sihanouk.

She's buying me clothes. A pretty cotton dress to take to Europe. New underwear. She walks through the lingerie department like a ghost. She's not my mother. My mother who used to slap her hand down on the counter at the cowering clerk: *We've been waiting twenty minutes! What does it take to get some service around here?*

My mother, who would drag all the hangers screeching down to the other end of the rod, then yank them back one by one so that their ruffles quivered: *Do you think I'm doing this for my health, girls? Don't be so picky!*

My mother standing at the door of the dressing room *Stop worrying! They can't see you!* blocking the corridor with her furious bulk. Then, *Nah! It doesn't do a thing for you!* as we stood foolishly before her with our stupid saddle shoes that she still made us wear. Our nerdy socks.

This is not my mother, this hollow being. She doesn't even know that I am there.

✿

We go to the Hot Shoppes on Wisconsin Avenue. I can't
believe we're even here. She never comes here. *It's really
crummy,* she always says. But here we are, in a booth, facing
one another across the turquoise table. My mother keeps her
sunglasses on and stares at me with her big, black, sunglass
eyes.

Then, without warning, she starts in on me.

*So what are you going to do? Are you just planing to live with
this—this Danny? Go off to Europe? Live with this guy? This
Danny, that you hardly even know? And then what? Some other
guy after that? What kind of life are you planning for yourself,
Martha?*

I don't know where this came from. I thought she liked
Danny. I stare at her.

What are your plans?

She's pecking at me like an angry bird. I don't know what
I did. She's been so tame!

And then, all of a sudden, she's quiet, and I see two tears
sliding down from under the black sharp triangles of her sunglasses. Her mouth changes shape, like a child's.

"I don't know what I'm going to do if they don't find
him."

19

THE SIDEWALK

IT'S JUST GETTING LIGHT. I'm still stoned from last night and the van smells horrible—like garbage and marijuana and old cigarette smoke. It's summer, and my father's still missing. We're in Spain.

Danny's lying next to me. I poke him but he keeps on sleeping. His curly black head reminds me of my sister hogging the pillow. It's hot in the van; and when I sit up I feel dizzy.

My stomach's all weird and gurgly inside. Maybe from that stuff we took. I haven't felt right since Paris. Suddenly I have to shit, but we parked right on the main street last night. We were so stoned we had to hang onto the sides of the buildings to get up the sidewalk.

"I've got to go to the bathroom," I say to Danny and he wakes up.

"What?"

"I've got to go! Really bad! Where am I supposed to go?"

"I don't know. Is it light yet?"

It's getting lighter every minute. The orange curtains make the light look different in here. Everything's kind of pinky.

"Go ahead," he tells me.

I'm naked. I pull on my yellow dress and my sneakers and get out of the van. Outside the air is cool. My legs are trembling. I feel like I might just shit right here, right in the middle of town, but I make my way up the block and head down a side street, hunched over like an old lady taking little steps.

The tall cementy-looking buildings go straight up from the sidewalk. I don't see anybody around. It's real quiet, nobody's awake. Some of the windows are barred with long black iron bars. So I just turn, take hold of the bars and, hanging back over the cobbled road with my dress hiked up right there in downtown Arenas del Mar, I shit and I shit and I shit. It keeps coming out of me, everything that's in me, everything I ate since Paris, rushing out in this one big hot lava flow. My legs are shaking. It doesn't even feel real, but it hurts. If I wasn't hanging onto the window bars I'd be clutching my own thighs with the pain. It's like a lumpy river, a river rushing over the rocks or something. I can picture what it is. It hurts.

Then it's done. I am hollowed out like a jack o' lantern. I am tiny and fragile and I'm shaking uncontrollably, shit streaked down my thighs. Gingerly I let go one hand from the bars and step away and look back at what I've done.

It's disgusting, yet somehow impressive. All that was in me. A big dark moundy lumpy pile of shit like a huge obscene helping of something: meatballs and gravy, choco-late ice cream, the dark dirt that's under the sand in the sand-box. Primeval.

I'm shaking. I don't think I can move.

But then I look up the street and I see some people com-ing down from the hills. They are coming toward me—three or four old Spanish ladies in black dresses. They have that squat look the women have in Spain with their black, cloaky, European clothes. They all look the same. They have sticks with them, and bags hanging off their arms and they are coming straight toward me.

I have to get out of here. They'll know it's mine. It smells really terrible; like something not even human; like rot.

I step away and head back down the street toward the main road.

Here they come.

As they come toward me and they grow more distinct, I walk away in my yellow cotton dress trying not to let the fabric touch me, walking with my legs a little apart so my thighs won't stick together. It's so gross.

I can hear them now. Chattering away in Spanish as they approach my pile.

I am a block away and almost to the main street where the van's parked. I look over my shoulder and see they have arrived at it. They all stop. They are chattering now more loudly in Spanish saying things that I don't understand and one of them prods at it with her stick and then they all look up at me, still chattering in their angry way like hens. They point their sticks at me now and they shake them.

I am weak and I am hollow and I am still shaking but I run, I run back to the van, open the door and throw myself inside. I don't want anyone to ever see me.

"Quick!" I say to Danny. "Quick!"

"God," he says, turning his head away. "What's that smell?" he asks.

20

WHERE I BELONG

"HE'S ALL RIGHT!" some lady shouts at me.

"What?"

"Are you Martha Dudman? You said your name is Martha Dudman?"

"Yeah."

"He's all right! Your father! We've been trying to reach you for a week now! Ads in the paper! Everything! He's all right! He's safe! He's home."

Around me, all the people in the line at the American Express office start talking to each other, cheering. A lady gives me a big pile of mail. Another one comes out with a newspaper pointing at an ad *Martha Dudman call home.* I don't know what they're talking about. My father?

✿

He's all right. I call the number later from a long distance telephone station full of dark wooden booths. Their voices, the voices of my family, are tiny and faraway. Outside it is bright and noisy. Barcelona on a summer afternoon. In here it is dim and cluttered with people. I hold the phone receiver tight to my ear. I can see Danny waiting for me, watching. I hear my father's voice, my mother. My sister's there. I can't understand what they're saying. Only that he's all right. They're all in Washington. What am I doing here? Their voices sound so tiny, far away. They're trying to tell me all about what happened but I feel like they're speaking a foreign language.

I try to feel happy that my father's safe, but I still feel sad. Because even if he's all right now he won't be there forever. It's like this door opened and I could see into the room beyond—the room which is the world without my father. And then the door shut and no, I don't have to go in there yet. But now I know about it, and I know I will inhabit it someday.

✿

My mother meets me at the airport in New York. Her face looks old to me.

"Martha!" she says and hugs me.

My father is in Maine. We'll go there, too.

"He was seriously ill," my mother tells me.

He's thin, but he is glad to see me. The island is the same. It's late summer. The sky and the trees and the field in front of our house are clean and bright with the September sunshine.

I sit at the table by the big front window and read my father's stories of his captivity in Cambodia that were published in the *St. Louis Post Dispatch.*

Reading his stories is like listening to him talk. He doesn't make his writing all big and important and boring—it's like he's telling a story. He puts in details, the smell of things, the sound of the men hurrying through the jungle, the rice in little bowls.

The people are real in his stories—the men who took him prisoner, the woman and the other reporter who were with him, the people he saw first, in the streets of Saigon. He tells about the war, sure, but it's the way he tells it that makes it real. The little girl in the red sweater waiting on the sidewalk—that's what will end the war. Not all the weary arguments pro and con. Not protests turning into be-ins at the Reflecting Pool.

There is so much power in just words. The way you pile them up on the page. The ones you leave in and the ones you take away. The objects and the people you describe. Those are the things that move us.

My mother leaves to go back to work, and my dad and I are in the house together. I walk around the island feeling very quiet. I don't want to talk to anyone, except my father. It's as if I'm the one recuperating from some terrible long illness; I feel thin and light. In the evening we play cribbage by the fire, and take a walk up to the post office and back again as it gets darker.

✿

We're walking down the main road. It's so quiet here in Maine, here on the island. There's some fog tonight and the air smells fresh and cool. It feels companionable and safe, walking with my father down this road which year after year is always the same—Natalie Beal's house on the right and the graveyard and the weedy tall grass on the left and then the Catholic church small and tidy with its dim small silence.

I want to tell my dad something. I'm so proud of him. All the stuff he's done. But then that also makes me feel small and unimportant; stupid for just hanging around and not doing anything worthwhile. Kids like me who grew up in Cleveland Park—we all had famous fathers. Fathers who were civil rights leaders or famous journalists or worked in the government or hotshot lawyers. And we were all raised to be something, too. We just weren't sure what it was. We knew we were all supposed to be famous. But famous for what? And I know my own limitations. I can barely remember where Egypt is! How am I supposed to be useful in the world? Walking here, with my father, in the island night, I can memorize each step, each word. I can describe it. I can figure out how it all fit together in the cosmos, but I can't do anything that would be worthwhile in my parents' eyes.

All I have is God and art and they are such small things in the useful pace of my parents' useful world.

"I'm not like you," I tell him. "I don't know about politics and wars and foreign policy. I just want to write poems and stories, but it seems so dumb."

"It isn't dumb, Martha," my father says. "Art, music, literature—they're what make us human. They're what make us different from monkeys."

♧

I sleep in the room I slept in as a child. I crank the window open so I can feel the black cold night, the Maine air coming in, and then I am all warm there in my bed with the blankets over me and in the morning I can hear the radio downstairs, the *CBS World News Round Up* on WDEA.

♧

One afternoon I run into one of the Cameron boys down by the dock and we start talking. He's fishing he tells me, just like his father. He's been to Vietnam and now he's home and the first day back his dad woke him up at six A.M. and told him he was going stern man, and now he has his own boat and four hundred traps.

It seems like a life beyond life. Like the kind of life you can only imagine: the island, the sky all the time, the water. Coming in tired and honest after the day, taking a big, hot shower, eating a big, hot supper, reading a book. Everything elemental and clean. And I want that, and I want to be done with my confusing life.

This feels like where I belong. This. Maine. The glint of the long grass beige-colored and silvery in the field. The dark spruce trees tall against the sky. The dock and the smell of the dock; bait and the boats at their moorings. Smoke puffed up into the sky from the chimney at my parents' house. The secret places in the woods, the warm rocks on the shore.

21

fUNKY

"This is where you live?"

My sister looks around at the squalid little house on the edge of Yellow Springs. We live off campus.

Danny and I are renting the third-floor room from Kenny Horowitz who has the whole rest of the house for his darkroom, his couch, his TV, his girlfriends, and his dog who isn't house-trained yet. Most of the time the dog shits on the kitchen floor which is covered with newspaper. You have to be careful where you step.

"There's a mouse in the sink," Annie tells me.

I look over. It's drowned, I guess, lying in a big pot that we used to cook bulgur. Nobody's done the dishes in a couple of days.

"Gross," Annie tells me.

She's right.

✿

The downstairs is kind of disgusting, but upstairs Danny and I have our own little slanty room in the attic with a mattress on the floor and two old chairs we painted yellow and a bureau in the corner that we share.

I'm taking poetry, creative writing, fiction, dance. He's studying psychology and sometimes in the evening we just sit up in our room and read our books and it's winter and we see the snow fall down outside our window. We have a little heater that glows orange.

Gary Snyder comes to Antioch and Danny and I go hear him read at Kelly Hall. Gary Snyder's poems are stark and simple. He knew Kerouac. I love the way he reads—like each word is important, each word—a stick on the ground, a stone, a dog—is only what he sees. After the reading we walk back across the frozen campus. Last fall's leaves blow around over the dead grass. There's something about the leaves, the poetry, and the night that make me feel achey and vague inside.

✿

"Remember when we talked about you writing songs?"

We're in our room. Danny's reading chemistry for a test he has tomorrow.

"You mean that time when I first met you?"

Last year.

"Yeah. And you said it was when you didn't think?"

"Yeah, I remember," he puts his book down in his lap and

looks at me. "You really liked the poetry, didn't you?" he asks me. "Gary Snyder?"

"I wish I could write like that. Well, not like that, but like me. I wish I could just write all the time."

I can hear the winter rain falling on the roof of our little house.

"You will," he says, and he puts his hand on the side of my face the way he does.

I wish that we could stay like this forever.

❧

Danny's friends Tag and Kiki come to visit. They're living on a farm in West Virginia. They dropped out.

"It's so fucked up here," Tag says.

I don't feel right with them. They were like stars or something when they had the band. You'd always see them around. Taller than anybody else, and with all that hair. Tag's hair is down past his shoulders and he has this scar on his lip that makes him look mean. Kiki is beautiful; she's really tall and skinny and she has long black hair. They're both from rich families, but they always wear old clothes. Not hip clothes, not like that. Just anything—red jeans and a black shirt with a button missing. An old gray sweater with a hole in the sleeve. But somehow it's cooler than anything else. They kind of scare me.

"But you'd like them," Danny tells me, "if you knew them more. They're really cool. Tag's like my brother. He just gets it."

"I just feel shy with them, and I never know what to say."

He puts his arms around me. "Don't worry. You just have to get to know them," Danny says.

✿

"Want to do some acid?" Danny asks me.

"I guess not," I tell him. I'm kind of sick of acid. There's so much surrounding that one little kernel when you're really *there*. The rest of it—the headlong rush going up, the long, endless craziness coming down, and then the sad part afterwards when the speed wears off—I'm kind of sick of it. Having to act straight when you're stoned. Having to have everything planned out so nothing freaks you. Not being able to remember any of what you figured out when you were tripping. You know everything, it seems like, when you're up there, but then, when you come down, it's all just gone. And anyway, there's stuff I want to do.

I'm taking a poetry class that I really like. I wrote this one poem and it was different than anything I'd ever written— the way it came out of me. It reminded me of certain moments in my life—dreamy moments, powerful moments. It seemed to come from somewhere deep inside me and yet the words were simple—anyone could understand it.

The teacher asked me to read it out loud. My hand shook as I held the paper so I had to sort of push my hand down on the table so they couldn't see. And after I'd read it there was a little silence; and I knew it was a silence I had made.

✿

"How was it?"

Danny's sitting in a chair in our room.

"It was okay," he says. "Actually it was pretty boring. It was too cold to go out so mostly we just hung around and watched television. We played a little music. I missed you the whole time. Hey, you want to go visit them? In West Virginia? On their farm?"

I don't know if I want to go, but I want to be with him. This is what it feels like I've always wanted. Somebody like him.

❧

The farm where Tag and Kiki are staying is just a shack really, on a big scrabbly piece of overgrown land with some bad fields up wobbly, rocky roads. They're renting it while they look for a farm to buy in West Virginia.

It's completely cold. The cold's like iron down here in West Virginia and the towns we drive through all look dirty and sad.

There's something wrong with my stomach. They don't have any water or electricity. We eat lentils cooked over a woodstove and it takes a really long time.

They tell this story they heard about how somebody found a hacked-up woman in the woods near here. Her husband killed her and ate some of the meat, and sold some as deer meat and left the rest of the body in the woods.

Late at night I have to go to the bathroom. My stomach's a mess. I go out through the snow to shit in the roofless outhouse. It's scary and dark and really really cold. I've got an oil lamp with me but it doesn't help much. The night around the mountain is dense and black. I think of the hacked-up lady and I kind of expect her to appear outside the outhouse with her ruined face.

✿

The next day we drive way up a long, bumpy road. Kiki rides in the back of the truck standing up with her hair blowing back wearing her red jeans. I want to be like her, but I never will be. It's not as cold now, with the sun out. The top of the mountain is wide and grassy like a beautiful dream. We sit on the grass and eat cottage cheese and homemade bread and canned kippers.

Danny turns to me and smiles. "You feeling better?"

I love him.

Maybe we should come live here, away from all the craziness in Yellow Springs. I could write. He could play his music. We could work on the farm.

There's a little abandoned farmhouse with a broken, ineffectual fence around it. We look in through the windows at the tiny rooms with the low ceilings. One of the rooms has cherries on the wallpaper. Somebody lived here once.

It's so far from everything. There's no ocean, just land in every direction, wooded parts and a stream cold and glittery and silver in the bright day.

Kiki goes off into the grass and pulls her pants down and pees right there, right with all of us watching. Nobody says anything. Her white ass sticking out of her red jeans. I could never be like her.

❀

Back in Yellow Springs it's cold and it's cold and it's cold and the house is dirty. We sit up in our room and I'm trying to read my book and the whole house smells. Danny's eating applesauce out of an orange plastic dish. He opens his chemistry book.

"Want to do spring quarter in West Virginia?"

"I guess so," I say.

I think we need to get out of Yellow Springs. Maybe if we were on the farm it would be better. Because I know I love him. It's just being here that makes it hard sometimes. This dirty house.

❀

I'm home for a week in April. I lie in my bed in my parents' house and I can hear my mother downstairs taking dishes out of the dishwasher. It's so clean.

The kitchen smells like laundry and she's ironing when I come in.

"Do you ever get depressed?" I ask my mother.

"Oh, sure," she says, and I'm surprised at how quickly she just says that. "I used to get really depressed. I called it the black hood. It was like this black hood came down over me and I couldn't see anything and I felt hopeless."

I try to picture it that way—a hood.

"What did you do?" I ask her.

She puts the iron down and looks at me. "I just kept going. That's what you do," she says, "you just keep going.

One foot in front of the other. And it does get better. After a while it gets better. And you know, as you get older, those moods are less intense. I hardly have them ever, anymore."

I don't know what to say. I can't imagine my mother being sad like that, like I get. I always knew she was emotional. She used to get so mad. But I thought it was something we did or didn't do that made her angry. Our messy rooms, my lousy grades at school. I always thought it was about me. I didn't think it might be inside her. I always thought of her as endlessly competent. Just striding forward, doing everything. Ramming her way through whatever brambles.

"It does get better, Martha," and she looks at me. "You'll be just fine."

✿

And I think she's right. Maybe everything's going to be okay. It doesn't have to be like Yellow Springs. It will be better when we're at the farm. We're going to plant crops.

22

FARM GIRL

I HATE TAG. We've been on the farm for a month. If you
want to call it a farm. It's really just a big old dilapidated
house like houses all over West Virginia, all falling down
with a broken roof and small, dark, bad rooms and no windows—just boards over some of them—and hardly any furniture. We keep our stuff in our knapsacks mostly or piled on
top. There's a barn, but it's no good either.

It's cold in West Virginia and it rains all the time. We have
to work anyway, even Jenny, who came with Tag's friend, Hal,
and just had an abortion. We've been clearing rocks out of the
field so we can plant. There's a big pile of muddy rocks on the
side where you're supposed to throw them only mostly I can't
throw them that far so I throw them in the general direction
and then Tag goes over in this real prancy way like he's making fun of me and picks up the rocks that have fallen short and

puts them on top of the pile. Sometimes at night I dream about rocks.

It's nothing like I imagined.

Today I'm planting onion seedlings. It's sort of sunny and Tag said it would be a good time to plant. I'm wearing one of my junk-store dresses from Ohio. I used to wear it to dances.

"A dress?" Tag said when I came out of the house.

"Yes," I answered in my most sarcastic voice. Like, *So?* But he doesn't care. He thinks I'm stupid. They all do, even Danny's starting to think so, though I know he loves me.

"You never hang out with the rest of us," he tells me. "You seem separate."

I *am* separate. How am I supposed to hang out with them? I don't know them. They're all different than I am. Kiki with her long hair. She'll do anything Tag tells her to. She thinks he's so great. And Tag with his mean face.

They all go take their clothes off and wash in the creek, but I won't go. I don't want Tag and Kiki and all the rest of them to see me naked. I don't even want Danny to see me naked. I'm too fat. And plus I'm bleeding. Something's wrong.

Jenny's bleeding too. She thinks maybe it's just from her abortion. Hal doesn't like her to take birth control pills because it's not natural. So now they can't have sex.

"But we went up to the ridge," she told me yesterday, when they came back, all smiling from their morning walk, "and had a really good eat-out."

At first I didn't know what she meant. And then I was embarrassed. You're not supposed to be embarrassed. It's one of the things that's not allowed.

Danny and I tried to make love later, but it wasn't very good. The bed we have in our room gets wet when it rains because the roof's all broken and the second floor isn't really finished off, so when it rains (and it's always raining) the rain comes down and gets on the bed. We've got this plastic thing rigged up now like a tent. It's better, because now we can't see the rats, but at night when we lie in bed, we can still hear them running back and forth upstairs.

"You want to?" he asked me.

I didn't, really. I'm too fat and I feel all dirty because there isn't any water except the creek and once in a while Mrs. Ray, who lives down the road, lets us take a shower at her house, but not too often.

But I said yes, so we tried to, only partway through I started bleeding again and when we finished Danny had blood on his penis and even though he acted like it was cool I could tell it bothered him.

I don't know what to do with my old tampons. I tried burning them in the stove, but they don't burn very well and Tag says they stink up the place. At first I put them in a bag and put them out on the back porch with the trash but then at night the rats came and in the morning there were bloody tampons dragged all around the backyard. If you want to call it that.

The next night Tag sat up all night, he told us, with a knife, waiting for the rats to come, but I don't think they did. They're not that dumb.

Mostly when I'm not working I read. It's cold, so I read in the kitchen by the woodstove while they all go out and splash in the creek or something. Mrs. Ray said there are snakes. You don't even see them but they'll bite you right on the ankle and then if you don't get to the hospital in time you die.

So I pretend that's why.

The kitchen's dirty. The walls are all sort of greasy-looking and black with smoke from the woodstove. We eat beans a lot and lentils and this sort of dark thick bread with raisins in it and no yeast. Oatmeal. "Where's the cookbook?" I asked Tag once. What a mistake. He made fun of me like I had to have this hoity-toity cookbook when all you do, *he* thinks, is just take a bowl and throw in a bunch of whole wheat flour and wheat germ and raisins and molasses and stuff and make this dark, thick bread that I chew on sitting in the kitchen with my book.

"You're always reading," he says, like it's not a good thing.

Tag thinks you should only read books with information in them. Books about how to plant crops, for example, books about how to wire a house.

They don't have electricity. Tag says we don't need it.

They do have a generator and one day a bunch of their friends came over and they put on the generator and played rock 'n' roll and then a bunch of other people came driving up in pickups and some young girls—teeny boppers from the town which is about twenty miles away—coming up to look at the hippies. They giggled the whole time and they were smoking cigarettes and they were so young and pale-looking with these little halter tops on and I wondered how we looked to them—Kiki with her long witchy hair and Danny with his little beard and Tag with his long hair and this weird gas station shirt he's started wearing. And me. What did I look like to them?

❀

The onions are all crooked. When I stand up, finally, the backs of my thighs are dirty from sitting in the dirt in the field planting those onions. My back hurts.

Tag comes over and takes a look at what I've done.

That's when I notice it's all crooked.

He doesn't say anything, but he has this disgusted look on his face like I'm no good for anything, and he just starts replanting everything I've done.

❀

"Let's take these two sick cunts into town and get them to a clinic," Tag says the next morning.

Jenny and I are both still bleeding. Maybe something didn't go right with her abortion.

We all drive into town in the pickup. Danny sits in back with me and holds my hand. There's a clinic that's open certain hours and we go there and we have to wait a long time in these green plastic chairs with other people. Tag and Hal and Danny go away and leave us there. There are ladies' magazines—*Woman's Day, Good Housekeeping*—on little tables and pamphlets about birth control. Most of the other women there look poor. Some of them, who are really young, have two or three kids already and they're pregnant. I don't want this life. Outside of the window I see the bare, sad hull of the downtown. There's an IGA and a drug store and some teenagers out on the street. They might be the girls who were at our farm last weekend, but I don't know. Even the side-walk looks dirty.

Then it's my turn, and they don't even have an examina-tion room, just a big linoleum hall with sections curtained off by screens on wheels. The doctor has black chest hair and his shirt isn't buttoned up all the way. He examines me quickly. Checks my breasts.

"My favorite part of the job," he tells me.

I don't say anything. He can treat me any way he wants. He's doing it for free.

"What's the matter?" I ask him. "I keep bleeding."

"Yeah," he says, straightening up. "I'm going to put you on a stronger dose of the Pill."

"Is that good for me?"

He looks at me. "That'll fix your problem," he says.

Then it's somebody else's turn.

We drive into Charlottesville. There's a record store that Tag wants to go to. They have old records and he knows the guy who owns it. But when we get there, nobody's in the store.

He lives there too, the guy. Tag calls up the stairs to him and then we all troop up into this tiny apartment. He's lying on the couch. He's really pale and he has this long blondish hair. Stuff lying all around.

"His works," Tag says, shaking his head in disgust. "I thought he was done with that."

Tag used to know a bunch of people who did smack, Kiki told me. He has no use for it.

✿

We get back in the truck.

"Are you okay?" Danny asks me.

In my hand I'm holding six little plastic packages of birth control pills. The new kind. They seem at odds with everything else—the pale, pinky-blue foil, each pill in its own little clear plastic jujube—not like the truck and the landscape of West Virginia. We're passing through broken farmland on the rough dirt road. All of it bumpy and funky and rotten and real. The birth control pills, the plastic and the color of them, the factory where they were made, all seem as if they come from another world.

23

LIKE HUMAN BEINGS

WE DRIVE UP to my parents' house in the middle of a hot spring day.

"Is this where you live?" Tag asks like he's surprised by it. Which is dumb, because I know he's really rich. He's from some fancy preppie family in Pennsylvania, even though he likes to act like he's just some poor guy off the farm. And Kiki's father is a senator or something. Her family lives in one of those huge houses in Chevy Chase, but she says, "Nice pad," as if it isn't.

Our street looks wonderful to me, but I can't show it. The trees almost meet overhead and all of the houses have porches.

The houses look close together, after all the vast, rotten, disorganized space in West Virginia. The gardens are carefully tended and they're full of flowers. The grass is perfect.

There's our house. 3409. And the Moores' house across the street, the Feldmans' house next door, and Mrs. Brown.

❖

By the time my parents come home, Tag and Danny have set up their equipment in the garage. There's a thick orange extension cord running from the kitchen across the backyard to the garage, and I can hear them out there. I'm in the house. I have taken a long shower in my own bathroom. I'm afraid to look at myself in the mirror. At the farm we only have one old scratched mirror, or you can look in the rearview mirror of the truck: your little face.

"What's wrong with your skin?" my mother asks me.

I have a huge pimple on my chin. The whole top's yellow, it's so big, and there are more of them on my forehead. I never had pimples like that. And I'm really fat. I weighed myself on my mother's scale. I've gained about twenty pounds. But I just stare back at her. "Nothing."

"Honey," she says and puts her arms around me.

"What's all that racket?" my father asks.

"They're in the garage," my mother tells him. "The boys. They're practicing."

All my parents' friends have kids like us. Living on farms in Vermont or West Virginia, playing in bands or staying at ashrams. Some of the parents themselves have become vegetarians or taken up yoga or started wearing dashikis. It's 1971.

"When are they going to stop?" my father asks.

✿

Tag and Kiki are staying in my sister's room. My parents let
me sleep with Danny in my room. Some parents won't do
that, but my parents are trying to be cool.

"I feel as if you're married," my mother says.

✿

On the second day my parents are at work.

"We'll get what we need and head back out tomorrow,"
Tag has told us.

I don't want to leave. I don't want to go back there. Those
dark smelly rooms. The rocky muck of the field. The rats
overhead. The smoky kitchen. That dark bread. I want to
stay here. I want to be in my parents' house. To hear my
mother downstairs taking dishes out of the dishwasher. To
hear my father typing in the night. I want to sleep in my own
room in my own four-poster bed and wake up and see the
bright trees outside my window and the blue and white wallpaper on my walls. And I want to read in a chair in the living
room, which is quiet and dim, the way it's always been. I
want to drive my parents' car, which works and doesn't get
stuck or have to grunt along in the slow lane because it only
goes in second gear. I want electricity. I want running water.
I want pretty dresses. I want a nice clean stove and my
mother's familiar pans that are all like my mother, hanging
from the copper rack my father made.

I want to sit at the kitchen table and see my father reading
the newspaper and the sunlight in the backyard.

I want to not smoke pot. Not take acid. Not sleep with people I don't know. Not have to pretend that things are cool when they are not cool. I want to be home.

🌀

I can hear Tag and Kiki and Danny talking in the kitchen. I come downstairs, determined to tell them. They're eating sandwiches, standing around my mother's table.

"Let's set the table and sit down and eat," I say.

Kiki looks amused. Tag looks up sharply. I hand him the paper napkins which are where my mother always keeps them on top of the oven; my mother with her tyranny of order which I've missed. He takes them, surprised. Danny is watching us.

"Set the table?" he asks me.

"Yes," I say bravely. "Yes. Let's set the table and sit down and eat like human beings."

I sound just like my mother.

Then Tag starts mincing around the table in this show-off way, taking dainty little steps with his big feet and folding the napkins just so in little triangles. "Like this?" he asks me.

I really hate him now.

"Yes!" I shout suddenly. "Yes! Just like that! That's how we do things here!"

Then I don't even want that—it's not enough—for him to fold the napkins, for him to mince about. For him to cut his sandwiches in half. I want him out of here—out of my house—out of my mother's home. Out with his orange extension cord and his tattery pants and his scar on his lip and his long black hair and his onion rows. Out.

"Get out of here!" I tell him, suddenly. Tell all of them, even Danny who's just standing there. He doesn't know what to do.

"Get out!" I yell. "I hate you, hate you, hate you!"

They stand there, frozen, staring at me. I've never done anything like this with them. Maybe I've never done it *ever.* Never yelled. It's boiling out of me, the yells I've got inside. Boiling. It's all the anger. I don't know what it is. But I know this. They don't belong here. Maybe I don't either, but I want them out.

✪

They all go toward the door. And though Tag makes a sarcastic face and shakes his head like I'm the crazy one and Kiki says a quiet, "Wow, that's pretty heavy, Martha," in a kindly voice—I don't care. Danny asks me, "Should I stay?" I shake my head. I want them out of here.

✪

When they're all gone the house is quiet. My parents won't be home for hours yet. I hear the truck start up out on the street, and then drive off with a quiet, homely sound. I pick up the napkins, unfold the ones he's folded. I put away the bread.

❧

"I'm not going back," I tell Danny later in my room. We're sitting on the bed together. He's not mad. He's never mad at me.

"How could I be?" he asks me. "You're just you."

I really love him, but I don't know what I want. To be with him. To be away from him. It's like my whole life I've been trying to find someone exactly like him. Somebody kind like this, and sweet—someone who loves me. And all the other boys, the rest of it, were just a warming-up or something. They didn't count. I feel sometimes as though he's me.

But I don't want to go back to the farm. I want to stay here, and then go back and finish college. Maybe I can be there in a different way. Maybe it wouldn't have to be all about dancing and getting high. Maybe I could learn things. Maybe other things could be like writing poems—could engage me that way—could seem as real as romance and my stunted search for life.

I still love Danny, but maybe what I really wanted was to get him; not to have him. In real life the romantic part, the part that gets stretched out in books and movies, is over so quick. And then all that's left is this: sitting on a bed together and talking like grown-ups.

I don't get how things work yet. I know there's a lot between who I am, who I always thought I would be, and what I will eventually become—and that somehow all those people are the same.

"Let's get out of here," I say to Danny. "I want to show you this place I used to go. It's right up the road."

We go out into the afternoon. The road is quiet. You can almost believe that you're not in the city; pretend the sound of the cars on Thirty-fourth Street is the sound of a river. We start walking up the road toward Rosedale, and I take his hand.

9 781416 568